SCOTT FORESMAN · ADDISON WESLEY

Mathematics

Grade 3

Practice Masters/Workbook

PEARSON

Scott
Foresman

Editorial Offices: Glenview, Illinois • Parsippany, New Jersey • New York, New York

Sales Offices: Parsippany, New Jersey • Duluth, Georgia • Glenview, Illinois
Coppell, Texas • Ontario, California • Mesa, Arizona

Overview

Practice Masters provide additional practice on the concept or concepts taught in each lesson.

ISBN 0-328-04955-7

15 16 V084 10 09

Ways to Use Numbers

Tell if each number is used to locate, name, measure, or count.

1.

2.

_____

_____

Sal   Yon   Frank   Joe   Kym   Lia

3. Who is fourth in line? _____

4. Write the ordinal number for Sal's place in line. _____

5. Reasoning If Joe leaves to find another book, who will be fifth in line? _____

Test Prep

6. Which ordinal number comes next? 42nd, 43rd, 44th,

A. 54th   **B.** 41st   **C.** 45th   **D.** 55th

7. Writing in Math Explain how a number can name something.

_____

_____

_____

_____

Numbers in the Hundreds

Write each number in standard form.

1.

2.

3.

_____   _____   _____

4. 700 + 30 + 6   _____

5. two hundreds, five tens, nine ones _____

Write the word name for each number.

6. 212   _____

7. 600 + 3   _____

Algebra Find each missing number.

8. 200 + 10 + _____ = 212   9. _____ + 70 + 1 = 971

Test Prep

10. Which is the missing number? 100 + _____ + 9 = 139

    A. 3   **B.** 13   **C.** 30   **D.** 33

11. **Writing in Math** Explain how the digit 7 can have different values.

_____

_____

_____

_____

_____

Name_____

Place-Value Patterns

Write each number in standard form.

1. [place-value blocks]

_____

2. [place-value blocks]

_____

3. **Number Sense** The largest giant jellyfish ever found was 7 ft wide and had tentacles that were more than 120 ft long. Draw place-value blocks to show 120 using only tens.

4. **Representations** Draw the place-value blocks needed to finish making 469.

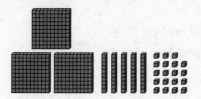

Test Prep

5. Which number has the same value as 4 hundreds, 7 tens, and 22 ones?

   A. 492   **B.** 472   **C.** 452   **D.** 427

6. **Writing in Math** Explain how you can use place-value blocks to show 100 in different ways.

_____

_____

_____

Name_____

Numbers in the Thousands

P 1-4

Write each number in standard form.

1.

2. 9,000 + 600 + 50 + 4

_____   _____

3. eight thousand, seven hundred fourteen   _____

Write each number in expanded form.

4. 1,069 _____

5. 2,002 _____

6. Reasoning Write a number that can be shown using
only thousands blocks or only hundreds blocks. _____

Test Prep

7. Fredrick wants to build 1,412 with place-value blocks. He
does not have any thousands blocks. How many hundreds
blocks will he use?

A. 41 **B.** 14 **C.** 4 **D.** 1

8. Writing in Math Explain how you know that 6,775 is the
correct answer to the clues below.

- My ones digit is 5.
- My thousands digit is one more than my ones digit.
- My hundreds digit is 7.
- My tens digit is the same as my hundreds digit.

What number am I?

_____

_____

_____

© Pearson Education, Inc. 3

Greater Numbers

Write each number in standard form.

1. seventy-five thousand, three hundred twelve   _____

2. one hundred fourteen thousand, seven   _____

3. 20,000 + 7,000 + 600 + 90 + 3   _____

4. 100,000 + 40,000 + 2,000 + 500 + 30 + 2   _____

Write each number in expanded form.

5. 73,581   _____

6. 100,317   _____

7. **Number Sense** Write a six-digit number in
   which the digit 4 has the value of 40,000.   _____

8. The area of Ethiopia is 437,600 square miles. Write the area
   of Ethiopia in expanded form.

   _____

9. The area of Israel is 8,550 square miles. Write the area of Israel in word form.

   _____

Test Prep

10. Which is the value of 3 in 328,469?

    A. 300   **B.** 3,000   **C.** 30,000   **D.** 300,000

11. **Writing in Math** Explain how 8 ten thousands can be equal
    to 80 thousands.

    _____

    _____

Read and Understand

Grandchildren Grandma Fee has four children. Each of her children has three children. Seven of Grandma Fee's grandchildren are boys. How many grandchildren does Grandma Fee have?

1. Tell the problem in your own words.

_____

_____

2. Identify key facts and details.

_____

_____

3. Tell what the question is asking.

_____

_____

4. Show the main idea.

5. Solve the problem. Write the answer in a complete sentence.

_____

6. Bakery Al's Pet Bakery baked 120 dog biscuits on Monday and 150 dog biscuits on Tuesday. It sold all but 30 of the biscuits and gave half the unsold biscuits to an animal shelter. How many biscuits did it sell? Write the answer in a complete sentence.

_____

© Pearson Education, Inc. 3

Name_____

Comparing Numbers

Compare the numbers. Use <, >, or =.

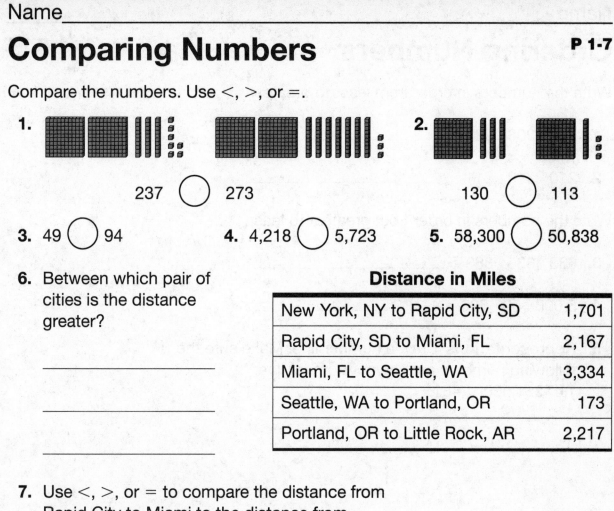

1. 237 ◯ 273

2. 130 ◯ 113

3. 49 ◯ 94

4. 4,218 ◯ 5,723

5. 58,300 ◯ 50,838

6. Between which pair of cities is the distance greater?

_____

_____

_____

Distance in Miles

New York, NY to Rapid City, SD	1,701
Rapid City, SD to Miami, FL	2,167
Miami, FL to Seattle, WA	3,334
Seattle, WA to Portland, OR	173
Portland, OR to Little Rock, AR	2,217

7. Use <, >, or = to compare the distance from Rapid City to Miami to the distance from Portland to Little Rock. _____

8. **Number Sense** Explain why 1,734 is greater than 175.

_____

_____

Test Prep

9. Which number is greater than 238,432?

A. 238,433   **B.** 23,899   **C.** 238   **D.** 238,431

10. **Writing in Math** Explain how to compare 8,563 and 8,699.

_____

_____

_____

Ordering Numbers

Write the numbers in order from least to greatest.

1. 216 208 222 _____

2. 210 219 211 _____

Write the numbers in order from greatest to least.

3. 633 336 363 _____

4. 5,000 50 500 _____

5. Representations Draw a number line. Make sure the
following numbers are on your number line:
1,472; 1,560; 1,481.

6. Write the river lengths in order
from least to greatest.

_____

_____

_____

World's Longest Rivers

River	Length (miles)
Amazon	4,000
Yangtze	3,964
Mississippi-Missouri	3,740
Nile	4,145

Test Prep

7. In which number does 4 have the greatest value?

A. 9,499 **B.** 4,391 **C.** 2,240 **D.** 1,944

8. Writing in Math Sara says the number with the most digits
is always greatest. Do you agree? Explain.

_____

_____

Number Patterns

Continue each pattern.

1. 15, 30, 45, _____, _____

2. 30, 24, 18, _____, _____

3. 3, 6, 9, _____, 15

4. 220, 230, 240, _____, _____

Use place-value patterns to find each sum or difference.

5. 890 − 300 = _____

6. 150 + 200 = _____

7. 470 − 350 = _____

8. 340 + 220 = _____

9. Joshua is raising fruit flies for a science project. At the beginning of the first day, he had 4 fruit flies. His fruit flies double in number each day. How many fruit flies does he have at the end of three days? _____

10. Representations Choose your own pattern. Draw a number line to show your pattern.

Test Prep

11. Which is 100 more than 7,399?

A. 7,400   **B.** 7,499   **C.** 8,399   **D.** 8,499

12. Writing in Math Mrs. Bradner has 30 tomato plants. She wants to plant the same number of plants in each row of her garden. Explain how she could decide the number of rows to plant.

_____

_____

_____

_____

Rounding Numbers

Round to the nearest ten.

1. 37   **2.** 92   **3.** 133   **4.** 2,219

_____   _____   _____   _____

Round to the nearest hundred.

5. 172   **6.** 929   **7.** 8,438   **8.** 5,555

_____   _____   _____   _____

9. Number Sense Tyrell says $750 is about $800. Sara says $750 is about $700. Who is correct? Explain.

_____

_____

10. Which two lakes have the same depth when rounded to the nearest hundred?

_____

11. Which lake has a depth of about 900 ft?

_____

Depths of the Great Lakes

Lake	Depth (feet)
Erie	210
Huron	750
Michigan	923
Ontario	802
Superior	1,333

Test Prep

12. Round 7,468 to the nearest hundred.

A. 7,400   **B.** 7,460   **C.** 7,470   **D.** 7,500

13. Writing in Math Explain how you would use a number line to round 148 to the nearest ten.

_____

_____

© Pearson Education, Inc. 3

PROBLEM-SOLVING SKILL

Plan and Solve

Pyramid Hector has made a pyramid of blocks.
He used eight blocks to build the bottom row of
the pyramid. All the rows are stacked on top of
each other. Each row has one less block than
the row it sits on. How many blocks did Hector
need to build his pyramid?

1. Finish the picture to help solve the problem.

2. What strategy was used to solve the problem?

_____

3. Write the answer to the problem in a complete sentence.

_____

Temperature The average temperature in Seattle, Washington,
during January is 45°F. February's average temperature is 49°F,
with 52°F in March and 58°F in April. May's average temperature is
12°F higher than March's temperature, and June's temperature is
11°F higher than April's. What are the average temperatures for
May and June in Seattle?

4. What strategy did you use to solve the problem?

_____

_____

5. Give the answer in a complete sentence.

_____

_____

6. What other strategy could you use to solve the Temperature problem?

_____

_____

Counting Money

Write the total value in dollars and cents.

1. _____

2. _____

3. Tell what bills and coins you could use to make $5.37 in two ways.

_____

_____

_____

4. Tell what coins you would use to show $0.37 using the
least amount of coins.

_____

Test Prep

5. Which does not mean 25 cents?

A. Quarter   **B.** $25   **C.** 25¢   **D.** $0.25

6. **Writing in Math** Explain how $0.60 can be shown two
different ways using only three coins each time.

_____

_____

Name_____

Making Change

List the bills and coins you would use to make change.
Then write the change in dollars and cents.

1. Seth paid for a $0.29 eraser with $0.50.

   _____

2. A new hair clip costs $1.60. Janice paid for a hair clip with
   two dollar bills.

   _____

3. **Reasoning** If pencils cost $0.26 each, could you buy four
   pencils with $1.00? Explain.

   _____

   _____

4. **Algebra** Alice bought an ice cream cone for
   $0.78. She got $0.02 change. How much money
   did Alice give the cashier?   _____

Test Prep

5. Martha used a dollar bill to pay for her $0.48 baseball card.
   Which does not show the proper change?

   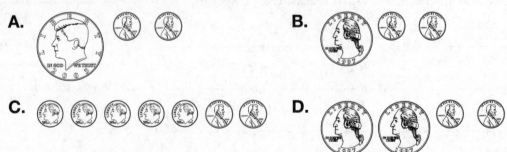

   A.   B.

   C.   D.

6. **Writing in Math** Braden and Bialy each bought a kazoo
   for $0.89. They each paid with a $1.00 bill. Explain two
   different ways to show their change.

   _____

   _____

Name_____

Look Back and Check

Pumpkin Seeds Ricardo planted 22 pumpkin seeds in hills. He planted 2 seeds in each hill. How many hills did he plant seeds in?

Esther solved the Pumpkin Seed problem. Check her work.

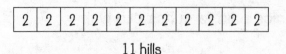

11 hills

1. Did Esther answer the right question? Explain.

_____

_____

2. Is her work correct? Explain.

_____

_____

Gardening Tedo makes $0.75 an hour weeding gardens. How much will he make if he works for four hours?

Joshua solved the Gardening problem. Check his work.

3. Did Joshua answer the right question? Explain.

Tedo's Pay

Hours	Pay
1	$0.75
2	$1.50
3	$2.00
4	$2.75

He will make $2.75 in four hours.

_____

_____

4. Is his answer correct? Explain.

_____

_____

Great Heights

There are many very tall mountains in the United States. The table shows the heights of a few of the tallest mountains.

Mountains in the United States

Mountain	Height (feet)
Mount McKinley	20,320
Mount Massive	14,421
Mount Rainier	14,410

1. Write the word form of the height of Mount Rainier.

   _____

   _____

2. Write the expanded form of the height of Mount Massive.

   _____

3. Order the heights from greatest to least.

   _____

4. Leonard would like to buy a fruit juice that costs $0.95. Leonard has five coins that equal that amount exactly. Tell what coins Leonard has.

   _____

   _____

Reba would also like to buy a fruit juice. She decides to buy one for herself and one for her friend Yvonne.

5. The two juices cost $1.90. If Reba pays for them with $10.00, how much change should she receive? _____

6. Tell two different ways Reba could receive her change.

   _____

   _____

Addition Properties

Find each sum.

1. $(4 + 2) + 1 =$ _____   **2.** $6 + (2 + 1) =$ _____

3. $6 + 1 + 5 =$ _____   **4.** $4 + 3 + 7 =$ _____

Write each missing number.

5. $7 + 2 = 2 +$ _____   **6.** $3 + 0 = 0 +$ _____

7. $(2 + 4) + 5 = 2 + ($ _____ $+ 5)$ **8.** $3 + (7 + 1) = 3 +$ _____

9. **Number Sense** Write a number sentence with 3 addends whose sum is 14.

_____

10. Alex played the Duck Pond, the Cake Walk, and the Hoop Shoot. How many tickets did he use?

_____

Games
Duck Pond .... 2 tickets
Face Painting .... 4 tickets
Cake Walk .... 3 tickets
Hoop Shoot .... 1 ticket
Wheel Spin .... 2 tickets

11. Patsy did the Cake Walk twice before she won a cake. Then she played the Wheel Spin one time and won a pencil. How many tickets did she use?

_____

Test Prep

12. Which property is shown by $5 + 2 = 2 + 5$?

   A. Identity Property   **B.** Associative Property

   C. Commutative Property   **D.** Distributive Property

13. **Writing in Math** Jake says adding 0 does not change a number. Is he correct? Explain.

_____

_____

Relating Addition and Subtraction

Complete each fact family.

1. 3 + 6 = _____

6 + _____ = 9

9 − _____ = 3

_____ − 3 = 6

2. 2 + 9 = _____

_____ + 2 = 11

11 − 2 = _____

_____ − 9 = 2

Find each missing number.

3. 7 + _____ = 13   **4.** 9 + _____ = 19   **5.** 8 + _____ = 12

6. Number Sense Write the fact family for 3, 9, and 12.

_____

_____

_____

_____

7. Write the fact family for the total number of dots on the domino.

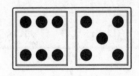

_____

_____

_____

_____

Test Prep

8. Which number sentence does not belong in the fact family?

A. 4 + 9 = 13   **B.** 13 − 4 = 9   **C.** 9 − 4 = 5   **D.** 9 + 4 = 13

9. Writing in Math Write a fact family with a sum of 17. Explain how you picked the addends.

_____

_____

_____

Find a Rule

Complete each table. Then write a rule for the table.

1.

In	7	13	4	12	0
Out	11	17	8		

_____

2.

In	16	9	4	18	3
Out	13	6	1		

_____

3.

In	16	31	27	62	99
Out	26	41	37		

_____

4.

In	57	39	71	22	19
Out	46	28	60		

_____

5. Number Sense Lako put in 12 and got out 17. Then she put in 1 and got out 6. What rule was she using?

6. Elton uses the rule Subtract 6 for his table. If he puts in 18, what will he get out?

_____

Test Prep

7. The rule for Stan's table is Subtract 4. Which number should he put in to get out 7?

A. 13   **B.** 11   **C.** 9   **D.** 3

8. Writing in Math Angel says the rule for this table is Add 0. Frank says the rule is Subtract 0. Who is correct? Explain.

In	6	14	31	29	0
Out	6	14	31	29	0

_____

_____

PROBLEM-SOLVING STRATEGY

Write a Number Sentence

Write a number sentence. Then solve. Write the answer in a complete sentence.

1. Hector bought 9 lb of dog food. His dog ate 3 lb in one week. How much dog food was left?

   _____

   _____

2. Janice pulled weeds for 2 hr on Saturday and 1 hr on Sunday. She watered the garden for 1 hr. How much time did she spend pulling weeds?

   _____

   _____

Heather has a new bead kit. It has directions for many different crafts. Help her decide how many beads to use. For 3–6, use the craft chart. Write your answer in a complete sentence.

Craft	Red Beads	Blue Beads
Necklace	10	12
Ankle chain	9	11
Key chain	24	16

3. How many beads in all does Heather need to make an ankle chain?

   _____

   _____

4. Heather will make a key chain and a necklace. How many blue beads will she use?

   _____

   _____

5. Heather has 17 blue beads. If she makes an ankle chain, how many blue beads will she have left?

   _____

   _____

6. How many beads in all does Heather need to make a key chain?

   _____

   _____

Mental Math: Break Apart Numbers

Find each sum using mental math.

1. 12 + 36 = _____

2. 42 + 37 = _____

3. 15 + 23 = _____

4. 17 + 42 = _____

5. 84 + 11 = _____

6. 52 + 35 = _____

7. **Number Sense** Ashton broke apart a number into 30 + 7. What number did she start with? _____

For 8 and 9, use the menu and mental math.

8. How much would an Orange Smoothie and a Peach Parfait cost?

_____

Drink Menu	
Strawberry Fizz	$0.45
Orange Smoothie	$0.31
Banana Blast	$0.11
Apple Cider Slush	$0.24
Peach Parfait	$0.46

9. Sarah wants two Apple Cider Slushes. How much will she pay?

_____

Test Prep

10. To break apart the number 42, which two numbers would you use?

    A. 40 + 20   **B.** 35 + 3   **C.** 40 + 2   **D.** 20 + 4

11. **Writing in Math** Explain how you would use mental math to add 14 + 71.

_____

_____

_____

Mental Math: Using Tens to Add

Find each sum using mental math.

1. 72 + 19 = _____

2. 36 + 28 = _____

3. 14 + 26 = _____

4. 17 + 49 = _____

5. 4 + 27 = _____

6. 55 + 37 = _____

7. Number Sense Jonah wants to add 43 + 19.
He added 43 + 20. What step should he take next? _____

In the United States House of
Representatives, the number of
representatives a state has depends
on the number of people living in
the state. Use mental math to find
each answer.

State	Representatives
California	52
New York	31
Texas	30
Florida	23

8. How many representatives do
California and Texas have
altogether?

_____

9. How many representatives do
Florida and New York have
altogether?

_____

10. Reasonableness Miles says 47 + 36 is the same as 50 + 33.
Is this reasonable? Explain.

_____

_____

Test Prep

11. Find the sum of 27 + 42 using mental math.

A. 69   **B.** 67   **C.** 62   **D.** 15

12. Writing in Math How does knowing 30 + 7 = 37 help you find 37 + 23?

_____

Estimating Sums

Round to the nearest hundred to estimate each sum.

1. 236 + 492 _____

2. 126 + 223 _____

Round to the nearest ten to estimate each sum.

3. 18 + 36 _____

4. 145 + 239 _____

Use any method to estimate each sum.

5. 167 + 449 _____

6. 387 + 285 _____

7. Number Sense April needs to estimate the sum of 427 and 338. Should she round to the nearest ten or to the nearest hundred to get the closer answer? Explain.

_____

_____

8. The flower shop just received a shipment of 432 roses. They need to fill an order for 273 roses. Use any method to estimate how many roses they will have left.

_____

Test Prep

9. Which of the following shows estimating 287 + 491 by using compatible numbers?

A. 200 + 500   **B.** 300 + 500   **C.** 280 + 400   **D.** 290 + 490

10. Writing in Math How can you use rounding to estimate 331 + 193?

_____

Overestimates and Underestimates

Estimate each sum by rounding. Then tell whether each
estimate is an overestimate or an underestimate.

1. 17 + 49 _____

2. 71 + 13 _____

3. 818 + 139 _____

4. 162 + 72 _____

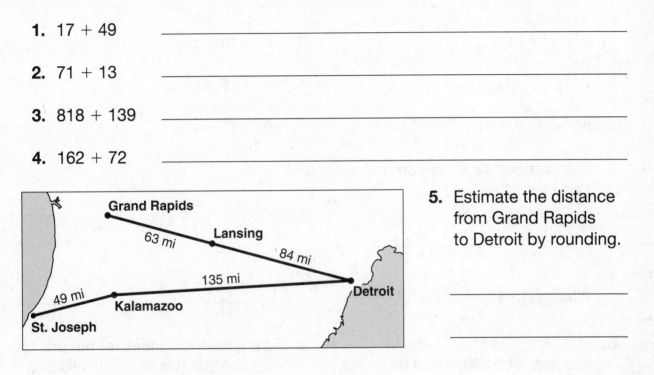

5. Estimate the distance
from Grand Rapids
to Detroit by rounding.

_____

_____

6. Did you underestimate or overestimate? _____

7. Stanton needs to travel from Detroit to St. Joseph. He says
he will drive more than 190 mi. Do you agree? Explain.

_____

Test Prep

8. Which is an underestimate?

  A. 89 + 139 is about 230.   **B.** 104 + 212 is about 310.

  C. 58 + 77 is about 140.   **D.** 437 + 15 is about 460.

9. Writing in Math Is it reasonable to say the sum of 146 and
149 is less than 300? Explain.

_____

_____

Mental Math:
Using Tens to Subtract

Find each difference using mental math.

1. $63 - 19 = $ _____

2. $47 - 18 = $ _____

3. $72 - 38 = $ _____

4. $61 - 25 = $ _____

5. $84 - 29 = $ _____

6. $80 - 11 = $ _____

7. **Number Sense** Gillian started solving $88 - 29$.
   This is what she did.

   $$88 - 29 = ?$$
   $$88 - 30 = 58$$

   What should she do next? _____

8. Mary has $84 in her bank account. She withdraws $67. Use mental math to find out how much she has left in her bank account.

9. Tiffany needs 63 tiles for her art mosaic. She has already collected 46 tiles. Use mental math to find how many more tiles she needs.

_____   _____

Test Prep

10. To solve $35 - 19$, Jack used $35 - 20$ and then

    A. added 1.   **B.** subtracted 1.   **C.** subtracted 9.   **D.** added 9.

11. **Writing in Math** Tell how to find $81 - 36$ using mental math.

_____

_____

_____

Mental Math:
Counting On to Subtract

Count on to find each difference mentally.

1. 43 − 16 = _____

2. 81 − 67 = _____

3. 72 − 16 = _____

4. 21 − 9 = _____

5. 33 − 18 = _____

6. 65 − 12 = _____

Algebra Count on to find the value of the missing number.

7. 37 + x = 59 _____

8. 17 + n = 72 _____

9. 48 + y = 67 _____

Victoria has saved 73 tokens from the toy store. The tokens can be turned in for prizes. Victoria checked the toy store's Web site to see what prizes were available. The chart at the right shows her choices.

Flying disc	19 tokens
Beach ball	26 tokens
Sunglasses	39 tokens
Beach towel	58 tokens

10. How many tokens will Victoria have left if she gets the beach towel?

_____

11. How many tokens would Victoria have left if she got the beach ball and the sunglasses?

_____

Test Prep

12. Which subtraction problem could be solved by thinking of

28 + _____ = 45?

A. 28 − 45　　**B.** 45 − 28　　**C.** 28 − 9　　**D.** 45 − 10

13. **Writing in Math** Write a missing addend addition sentence to help solve 78 − 49. Explain how you would use it.

_____

_____

_____

Estimating Differences

Round to the nearest hundred to estimate each difference.

1. 236 − 119 _____   **2.** 558 − 321 _____

Round to the nearest ten to estimate each difference.

3. 677 − 421 _____   **4.** 296 − 95 _____

Use any method to estimate each difference.

5. 667 − 329

_____

6. 882 − 651

_____

7. Number Sense Fern rounded to the nearest ten to find 548 − 132. She thought 540 − 130 = 410. Do you agree? Explain.

_____

8. Hector's music teacher requires 450 min of practice each month. Hector practiced 239 min the first three weeks this month. Estimate how many minutes he has left to practice.

_____

Test Prep

9. Which is not a compatible number for 76?

A. 80   **B.** 75   **C.** 70   **D.** 60

10. Writing in Math Below are Kate's and Kirk's estimates for 177 − 129. Whose answer is closer to the actual answer? Explain.

Kate: 180 − 130 = 50
Kirk: 200 − 100 = 100

_____

PROBLEM-SOLVING SKILL

Writing to Explain

Snacks The school is going to give each student at Rose Elementary School a granola bar for a snack during field day. There are 758 students. They have already purchased 439 granola bars. About how many more granola bars do they need?

1. Is an exact answer or an estimate needed for this problem? Explain.

_____

2. What operation is needed to solve this problem? Why?

_____

3. What is the answer?

_____

_____

4. Use mental math to find the exact number of granola bars they still need to purchase.

_____

5. Draw a picture to show why you subtracted to solve the problem.

6. Writing in Math Explain how the digit 1 can have different values in 111.

_____

_____

_____

_____

Name_____

Fire Trucks

For 1–3, use the Key Facts: Ladder Trucks chart.

1. Use mental math to find the number of people who can sit in three fire trucks.

_____

2. Write the word name for the length of the hose on a ladder truck.

_____

3. Estimate the difference between the maximum ladder height and the truck length. Explain how you estimated.

_____

_____

_____

KEY FACTS Ladder Trucks	
• Truck width	8 ft
• Truck length	37 ft
• Maximum ladder height	105 ft
• Water spray per minute	1,500 gal
• Seating	6 people
• Hose length	1,000 ft
• Hose width	5 in.

For 4 and 5, use the Firefighting Models chart.

4. Marcy has $10. Does she have enough money to buy an aerial ladder and a fire chief car? Why or why not?

_____

_____

_____

Firefighting Models

Model	Price
Pumper	$5
Aerial ladder	$8
Fire chief car	$4
Rescue unit	$6

5. Diego bought one of each type of model. How much money did he spend?

_____

Name_____

Adding Two-Digit Numbers

1. $\begin{array}{r} 73 \\ + 19 \\ \hline \end{array}$
2. $\begin{array}{r} 16 \\ + 48 \\ \hline \end{array}$
3. $\begin{array}{r} 52 \\ + 39 \\ \hline \end{array}$
4. $\begin{array}{r} 28 \\ + 8 \\ \hline \end{array}$

5. $\begin{array}{r} 62 \\ + 19 \\ \hline \end{array}$
6. $\begin{array}{r} 14 \\ + 32 \\ \hline \end{array}$
7. $\begin{array}{r} 59 \\ + 27 \\ \hline \end{array}$
8. $\begin{array}{r} 36 \\ + 26 \\ \hline \end{array}$

9. $58 + 28 =$ _____

10. $13 + 72 =$ _____

11. **Number Sense** Tad's place-value blocks are shown at the right. What two numbers is he adding?

_____

12. What is the answer to Tad's problem?   _____

13. Esther swam 18 laps on Monday and 13 laps on Tuesday. How many laps did she swim in all?   _____

14. Write an addition sentence with the sum of 42. One of the addends must have a 4 in the ones column.

_____

_____

Test Prep

15. Which is the sum of $72 + 25$?

    A. 99   **B.** 97   **C.** 90   **D.** 79

16. **Writing in Math** How can estimating help you add two-digit numbers?

_____

_____

Models for Adding Three-Digit Numbers

Write each problem and find the sum.

1.

_____

2.

_____

3. Number Sense Matthew wants to show 137 + 429 with place-value blocks. He has enough hundreds and ones blocks, but he only has 4 tens blocks. Can he show the problem? Explain.

_____

4. Museum A has 127 steps. Museum B has 94 steps. Museum C has 108 steps. How many steps do Museums A and B have combined?   _____

5. How many steps do all three museums have?   _____

Test Prep

6. Use the information in Exercise 4. How many steps do Museums A and C have combined?

A. 254 steps   **B.** 235 steps   **C.** 216 steps   **D.** 188 steps

7. Writing in Math Write a number sentence for the place-value blocks below. Find the sum.

_____

Name_____

Adding Three-Digit Numbers

1.   329
   + 468

2.   148
   + 231

3.   555
   + 777

4.   718
   + 29

5.   152
   + 535

6.   396
   + 428

7.   592
   + 168

8.   633
   + 210

9. 536 + 399 = _____

10. 319 + 791 = _____

Long Jumpers

Animal	Distance (feet)
Flying dragon	100
Flying fish	328
Sugar glider	300

11. What is the total maximum distance that the flying
    dragon and the flying fish can jump together?   _____

12. What is double the sugar glider's maximum
    gliding distance?   _____

Test Prep

13. Find the sum of 163 + 752.

    A. 895   **B.** 915   **C.** 925   **D.** 929

14. **Writing in Math** Write an addition story for two 3-digit
    numbers. Write the answer to your story.

    _____

    _____

    _____

    _____

Name_____

Adding Three or More Numbers

1.	36	2.	142	3.	524	4.	716
	29		297		97		12
	+ 12		+ 116		+ 190		+ 149

5.	156	6.	241	7.	98	8.	420
	561		421		312		318
	+ 213		+ 124		+ 175		+ 196

9. **Estimation** Estimate the sum of 327 + 419 + 173. _____

10. **Number Sense** Justine has 162 red buttons, 98 blue buttons, and 284 green buttons. She says she knows she has more than 500 buttons without adding. Do you agree? Explain.

_____

_____

11. Carlos ate 1 oz bran flakes, 1 banana, 1 c whole milk, and 1 c orange juice. How many calories did he eat?

_____

Breakfast

Food	Amount	Calories
Bran flakes	1 oz	90
Banana	1	105
Orange juice	1 c	110
Whole milk	1 c	150

Test Prep

12. Kyle has 378 pennies, 192 nickels, and 117 dimes. How many coins does he have altogether?

A. 495   **B.** 570   **C.** 677   **D.** 687

13. **Writing in Math** Write an addition problem with 3 addends in which you regroup once to solve.

_____

PROBLEM-SOLVING STRATEGY

Draw a Picture

Finish the picture for each problem. Write the answer in a complete sentence.

1. Mr. Harper is making a walkway with steppingstones in his garden. He uses a pattern of 1 steppingstone, then 2. How many groups of that pattern can he build with 15 steppingstones?

_____

_____

Draw a picture to solve each problem. Write the answer in a complete sentence.

2. The balloon man at the circus has slippery fingers. Each time he blows up 5 balloons, 3 of them slip from his hands and fly away. How many balloons will he have to blow up before he is holding 8 balloons?

_____

_____

3. Olive's pet cricket jumps 2 in. one day and 3 in. the next. If this pattern continues, how many days will it take Olive's cricket to jump 12 in.?

_____

Regrouping

Regroup 1 ten for 10 ones. You may use place-value blocks
or draw a picture to help.

1. 67 = 6̸ tens, 7̸ ones

   67 = _____ tens, _____ ones

2. 30 = 3̸ tens, 0̸ ones

   30 = _____ tens, _____ ones

Regroup 1 hundred for 10 tens. You may use place-value
blocks or draw a picture to help.

3. 317 = 3̸ hundreds, 1̸ ten, 7 ones

   317 = _____ hundreds, _____ tens, _____ ones

4. 420 = 4̸ hundreds, 2̸ tens, 0 ones

   420 = _____ hundreds, _____ tens, _____ ones

5. **Writing in Math** Draw two ways to show 128 using place-value blocks.

Test Prep

6. 4 hundreds, 2 tens, 17 ones =

   A. 4,217   **B.** 427   **C.** 437   **D.** 431

7. **Writing in Math** Heidi says 381 = 2 hundreds, 7 tens, 11 ones.
   Do you agree? Explain.

   _____

   _____

Subtracting Two-Digit Numbers

1.	71 − 10	2.	65 − 18	3.	19 − 17	4.	35 − 11

5.	91 − 38	6.	40 − 26	7.	21 − 17	8.	83 − 56

9. 89 − 66 = _____   **10.** 52 − 38 = _____   **11.** 63 − 35 = _____

12. Stanton used the addition sentence 21 + 16 = 37 to check
his work. Write two subtraction problems that Stanton
could have been checking.

_____

13. The tree farm had 65 shade trees for sale. It sold 39 of the
trees. How many trees did it have left?

_____

_____

Test Prep

14. Find the difference of 76 − 38.

A. 42   **B.** 38   **C.** 36   **D.** 32

15. Writing in Math Bethany has 40 apples. Write a
subtraction story about the apples that would require
regrouping. Then write the answer in a complete sentence.

_____

_____

_____

_____

Name_____

Models for Subtracting Three-Digit Numbers

Find each difference. You may use place-value blocks or draw a picture to help.

1.   321
   − 176

2.   716
   − 99

3.   543
   − 268

4.   133
   − 127

5. 613 − 299 = _____

6. 401 − 102 = _____

7. 836 − 729 = _____

8. 634 − 277 = _____

9. **Number Sense** Tyson wanted to solve 638 − 152.
   He began by finding 6 − 5. Tell what Tyson did wrong.

_____

_____

10. What was the difference between the
    greatest and the least number of pages read?

    _____

11. Did Helen read more pages than
    Francis and Lance combined?
    How much more or less did Helen read?

Reading Record

Name	Pages Read
Alexander	716
Carrie	614
Francis	337
Helen	791
Lance	448

Test Prep

12. Simien collected 124 cans for the food drive. Jane collected
    79 cans. How many more cans did Simien collect?

    A. 55   **B.** 52   **C.** 45   **D.** 42

13. **Writing in Math** Write a subtraction sentence in which you
    would have to regroup hundreds.

_____

Subtracting Three-Digit Numbers

1.
```
  491
- 216
```

2.
```
  712
- 328
```

3.
```
  127
-  35
```

4.
```
  721
- 153
```

5.
```
  209
-  16
```

6.
```
  918
- 436
```

7.
```
  555
- 164
```

8.
```
  422
- 244
```

9. 621 − 411 = _____

10. 318 − 129 = _____

11. 582 − 276 = _____

12. 111 − 89 = _____

13. **Number Sense** Alice found 812 − 413 = 399. She added 812 + 399 to check her work. What did she do wrong?

_____

_____

14. How much taller is the coast redwood than the coast Douglas fir?

_____

Tree Heights

Tree	Height (feet)
Coast redwood	321
Coast Douglas fir	281
Common bald cypress	83

15. What is the difference in height between the coast redwood and the common bald cypress? _____

Test Prep

16. Which is the difference of 811 − 376?

   A. 425   **B.** 435   **C.** 436   **D.** 515

17. **Writing in Math** Kia found the difference of 378 − 299 to be 179. Is she correct? Explain.

_____

_____

Subtracting Across Zero

1.	406 − 28	**2.**	300 − 211	**3.**	501 − 268	**4.**	707 − 77

5.	605 − 219	**6.**	800 − 579	**7.**	901 − 728	**8.**	704 − 95

9. 404 − 305 = _____

10. 501 − 223 = _____

11. Patricia estimated that 439 − 186 would be close to 300.
Do you agree? Explain and solve the problem.

_____

_____

12. There are 600 ears of corn for sale at the produce market.
At the end of the day there are 212 ears left. How many
ears of corn were sold?

_____

13. Party Palace has an order for 505 party favors. It packaged 215
favors in the morning and 180 favors in the afternoon. How
many party favors does it still need to package to fill the order?

_____

Test Prep

14. 3 hundreds, 10 tens, 6 ones =

A. 316   **B.** 306   **C.** 416   **D.** 406

15. **Writing in Math** Explain how you can estimate to tell
whether 433 − 147 = 286 is reasonable.

_____

_____

PROBLEM-SOLVING SKILL   P 3-11

Exact Answer or Estimate?

Were less than 50 sack lunches eaten
during the week?

Sack Lunches	
Monday:	▢ ▢ ▢ ▢
Tuesday:	▢
Wednesday:	▢ ▢ ▢ ▢ ▢
Thursday:	▢ ▢ ▢
Friday:	▢ ▢ ◹
Each ▢ = 2 sack lunches.	
Each ◹ = 1 sack lunch.	

1. What do you know?

    _____

    _____

    _____

    _____

2. What are you trying to find?

    _____

    _____

3. What operation will you use? _____

4. Is an estimate enough? Explain.

    _____

    _____

    _____

5. Solve the problem. Give your answer in a complete sentence.

    _____

    _____

6. How many more sack lunches were eaten on Wednesday
   than on Thursday?

    _____

Adding and Subtracting Money

1. $7.29
   − 1.03

2. $3.50
   + 2.91

3. $6.00
   − 2.59

4. $17.99
   − 13.86

5. $20.00
   − 18.42

6. $12.04
   + 3.16

7. $4.21
   + 3.99

8. $6.18
   − 3.19

9. $7.83 + $0.62 = _____

10. $16.02 − $5.19 = _____

11. $18.21 + $14.36 = _____

12. $27.36 − $15.29 = _____

13. Liz gets paid $4.75 each day for delivering newspapers. How much money will she have after delivering newspapers for 3 days?

_____

14. Liz saved her money for 3 days to buy new tennis shoes for $16.98. Tell how much money she still needs or how much she will have left over.

_____

Test Prep

15. Sam paid for a notebook that costs $0.76 with a $1.00 bill. What was his change?

   A. $0.24   **B.** $0.42   **C.** $0.75   **D.** $0.34

16. **Writing in Math** Austin paid for $4.77 worth of groceries with a $5.00 bill. Could he have received a quarter with his change? Explain.

_____

_____

_____

Choose a Computation Method

Use mental math, paper and pencil, or a calculator to solve.

1. $\begin{array}{r} 716 \\ -\ 310 \\ \hline \end{array}$

2. $\begin{array}{r} 11,234 \\ -\ 2,378 \\ \hline \end{array}$

3. $\begin{array}{r} \$4.76 \\ +\ 2.25 \\ \hline \end{array}$

4. $\begin{array}{r} 720 \\ -\ 319 \\ \hline \end{array}$

5. $\begin{array}{r} \$32.61 \\ +\ 19.86 \\ \hline \end{array}$

6. $\begin{array}{r} 780 \\ -\ 298 \\ \hline \end{array}$

7. $\begin{array}{r} 400 \\ -\ 312 \\ \hline \end{array}$

8. $\begin{array}{r} 204,516 \\ +\ 307,629 \\ \hline \end{array}$

9. 158 + 269 = _____

10. $13.00 − $9.57 = _____

11. **Number Sense** Would you use mental math to solve
2,984 + 1,997 + 406? Explain.

_____

_____

12. Pauline subtracted 3,162 − 1,498 as shown.

What did Pauline do wrong?

$\begin{array}{r} 3,162 \\ -1,498 \\ \hline 2,664 \end{array}$

_____

_____

Test Prep

13. Find 650 − 298.

A. 352   **B.** 350   **C.** 302   **D.** 358

14. **Writing in Math** Solve this problem with pencil and paper:
2,593 + 1,389. Tell one way you could check your answer.

_____

_____

_____

Equality and Inequality

Compare. Write <, >, or = for each $\bigcirc$.

1. 20 $\bigcirc$ 13 + 9

2. 14 − 7 $\bigcirc$ 16 − 8

3. 32 + 5 + 3 $\bigcirc$ 40

4. 268 − 112 $\bigcirc$ 112 + 268

5. \$3.29 + \$7.16 $\bigcirc$ \$10.50

6. 1 + 2 + 3 $\bigcirc$ 3 + 2 + 1

Find three whole numbers that make each number sentence true.

7. 15 + x > 18　　　　　x = _____

8. 375 − n < 200　　　　　n = _____

9. Which two animals are able to spend an equal number of minutes under water?

_____

_____

Average Breath-Holding Time Underwater

Animal	Minutes
Hippopotamus	15
Muskrat	12
Platypus	10
Porpoise	15
Sea otter	5

10. The muskrat can hold its breath for a greater amount of time than which two animals?

_____

Test Prep

11. Which number does not make the number sentence

26 + y > 30 true?

A. 10　　　　**B.** 4　　　　**C.** 7　　　　**D.** 100

12. **Writing in Math** Write a number sentence with two expressions that equal each other.

_____

_____

PROBLEM-SOLVING APPLICATIONS

Bow-Wow Facts

The American Kennel Club (AKC) is a national group that has lots of information about dogs, including ways to keep dogs healthy, facts about different kinds of dogs, and rules in dog shows.

1. The AKC says that a male Alaskan malamute show dog should weigh about 85 lb and that a female should weigh about 10 lb less. About how much should a female weigh?

   _____

2. The average female St. Bernard show dog weighs about 145 lb. The average male St. Bernard weighs about 20 lb more. About how much does the average male St. Bernard show dog weigh?

   _____

3. Suppose you have 3 greyhounds for pets. They weigh 56 lb, 72 lb, and 63 lb. What is their combined weight?

   _____

4. Suppose you want to buy some 40 lb bags of dog food at $33.00 per bag, including tax. If you had $100.00, could you buy 3 bags? Explain.

   _____

   _____

5. Suppose you wanted to buy some dog toys and supplies. The total cost is $127.73. To find how much change you would get from $150.00, would it be best to use mental math, pencil and paper, or a calculator? Explain.

   _____

   _____

   _____

Time to the Half Hour and Quarter Hour

Write the time shown on each clock in two ways.

1.

_____

_____

2.

_____

_____

3. Number Sense Would it take closer to a minute
or an hour to clean your room?   _____

4. The school bus stops at Randy's bus stop at 8:15 A.M.
Randy arrived at the bus stop at a quarter after 8:00. Did
he miss the bus? Explain.

_____

_____

Test Prep

5. Which does NOT describe 5:15?

A. five forty-five   **B.** quarter after five

C. five fifteen   **D.** fifteen minutes after five

6. Writing in Math Explain the difference between A.M. and P.M.

_____

_____

_____

Name_____

Time to the Minute

Write the time shown on each clock two ways.

1.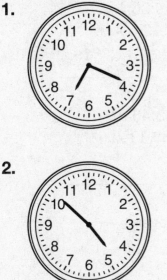

_____

_____

2.

_____

_____

3. **Number Sense** If Patricia won the race, who finished last?

_____

4. **Reasoning** Who finished closest to 8:00 P.M.?

_____

Marathon Run

Runner	Finish Time
Abbot, Frank	7:55 P.M.
Darling, Jasper	12:18 A.M.
Lawston, Ceilia	10:32 P.M.
Olson, Patricia	6:17 P.M.
Volst, Sandra	8:19 P.M.

5. Did Ceilia Lawston finish before or after 10:40 P.M.?

_____

Test Prep

6. Jan's alarm clock goes off at 12 minutes before 7:00 A.M. How many minutes past 6:00 A.M. is that?

   A. 48   **B.** 21   **C.** 19   **D.** 12

7. **Writing in Math** Write the time you are finished with school each day in two ways.

_____

Elapsed Time

Find the elapsed time.

1. Start Time: 6:00 P.M.
   End Time: 7:15 P.M.

   _____

2. Start Time: 9:30 A.M.
   End Time: 11:55 A.M.

   _____

3. Start Time: 4:15 P.M.
   End Time: 7:22 P.M.

   _____

4. Start Time: 3:48 P.M.
   End Time: 8:11 P.M.

   _____

5. Tara's baby sister naps between 12:45 P.M. and 2:30 P.M. every
   day. How long is the baby's nap?

   _____

6. Write the beginning time and the ending time of your
   school day. What is the elapsed time of your school day?

   _____

   _____

Test Prep

7. Which is the elapsed time?   Start Time: 1:01 P.M.
                                    End Time: 3:02 P.M.

   A. 3 hr 1 min   **B.** 2 hr 12 min

   C. 2 hr 2 min   **D.** 2 hr 1 min

8. **Writing in Math** Would you rather have your recess last
   from 10:30 A.M. to 10:45 A.M. or from 10:45 A.M. to
   11:10 A.M.? Explain.

   _____

   _____

Name_____

Using a Calendar

1. Write the ordinal number for the month of March. _____

2. Number Sense How many months are in
two years? _____

Use the calendar for Exercises 3–7.

3. How many Sundays were in June?

_____

June 2002						
S	**M**	**T**	**W**	**T**	**F**	**S**
						1
2	3	4	5	6	7	8
9	10	11	12	13	14	15
16	17	18	19	20	21	22
23	24	25	26	27	28	29
30						

4. What day of the week was June 1?

_____

5. Miguel left for vacation June 11. He returned
home June 25. How many weeks was he gone? _____

6. Reasoning On what day of the week was the
Fourth of July celebrated? _____

7. Mr. Evans began to paint his house on June 14.
It takes him nine days to finish the job. On what
date did he finish painting the house? _____

Test Prep

8. Macy's piano lessons begin the 1st of September. She has
lessons for eight months. Which is the last month of her
piano lessons?

A. March   **B.** April   **C.** June   **D.** July

9. Writing in Math Do some people live eight centuries or
eight decades? Explain.

_____

_____

_____

Using Tally Charts to Organize Data

Phillip took a survey to find out the age of each person in his class.

Ages of Classmates

Age	Tally	Number
8 years	ꜰꜰꜰꞁ	6
9 years	ꜰꜰꜰ ꜰꜰꜰ ǁ	12
10 years	ǁǁǁ	3

1. How old are most of Phillip's classmates? _____

2. How many students are in Phillip's class? _____

3. How many more students are 8 years old than 10 years old? _____

4. There are twice as many 9-year-olds than what age group? _____

5. Are there more or fewer students in Phillip's class than in your class?

_____

_____

Test Prep

6. Which shows the number for ꜰꜰꜰ ꜰꜰꜰ ꜰꜰꜰ ꜰꜰꜰ ǁǁǁǁ?

   A. 14   **B.** 24   **C.** 25   **D.** 44

7. **Writing in Math** Name five different topics that can be used to take a survey.

_____

_____

_____

Name_____

Using Line Plots to Organize Data

Ms. Temple, the librarian, asked students
to keep track of the number of books they
read in one month. The line plot at the right
shows the results she received.

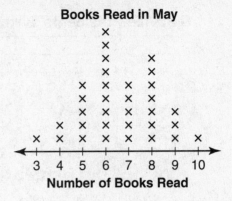

Books Read in May

Number of Books Read

1. What is the range of the data?

   _____

2. How many students kept track of their
   reading for Ms. Temple?

   _____

3. How many students read 7 books?   _____

4. How many fewer students read
   8 books than 6 books?   _____

5. How many books were read by
   3 of the students?   _____

6. What is the mode for the data?   _____

7. **Reasoning** Janice says the girls read more books than the
   boys. Can she prove her statement with the data on this
   line plot? Explain.

   _____

Test Prep

8. Which of the following is the difference between the
   greatest and the least numbers in the data?

   A. Mode   **B.** Median   **C.** Mean   **D.** Range

9. **Writing in Math** Phyllis says you can plot favorite colors of
   a sixth-grade class on a line plot. Do you agree? Explain.

   _____

   _____

Reading Pictographs and Bar Graphs   P 4-7

U.S. Vice-Presidents' Birthdays

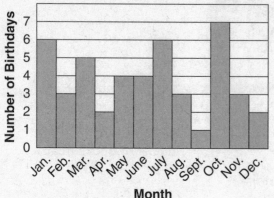

Month

U.S. Presidents' Birthdays

January	🚶🚶
February	🚶🚶
March	🚶🚶🚶
April	🚶🚶
May	🚶
June	🚶
July	🚶🚶
August	🚶🚶
September	🚶
October	🚶🚶🚶
November	🚶🚶🚶
December	🚶🚶

Key

Each 🚶 stands for 2 presidents.

Use the bar graph for 1 and 2.

1. Which month has 5 birthdays?

_____

2. Three months have the same number
of birthdays. Which months are they?

_____

Use the pictograph for 3 and 4.

3. How many months have the birthdays of
4 presidents?   _____

4. Number Sense If August had 3 more figures,
how many birthdays would be represented?   _____

Test Prep

5. Which of the following do pictographs and bar graphs represent?

A. Ideas   **B.** Directions   **C.** Data   **D.** Estimation

6. Writing in Math Look at both of the graphs above. What do you
notice about the number of birthdays during October as
compared to the number of birthdays during any other month?

Name_____

Writing to Compare

Read the tally charts and look for comparisons.

**Favorite Subjects
Mrs. James's Class**

Subject	Tally	Number
Math	☰☰☰ |||	8
Science	||||	4
Reading	☰☰☰ ||	7
Social studies	☰☰☰		6

**Favorite Subjects
Mr. Grey's Class**

Subject	Tally	Number
Math	☰☰☰ ||	7
Science	☰☰☰	5
Reading	☰☰☰		6
Social studies	☰☰☰		6

1. Write two statements that compare the favorite subjects of the students in the two classes.

_____

_____

_____

_____

2. Two students were absent from school the day Mr. Grey's class took this survey. How many students does Mr. Grey teach?   _____

3. Two students in Mrs. James's class chose music and one student chose art. How many students are in Mrs. James's class?   _____

4. Writing in Math How can graphs and charts help us make comparisons?

_____

_____

_____

Graphing Ordered Pairs

Write the ordered pair that describes the location of each attraction.

1. Elephants

   _____

2. Train station

   _____

3. Hippos

   _____

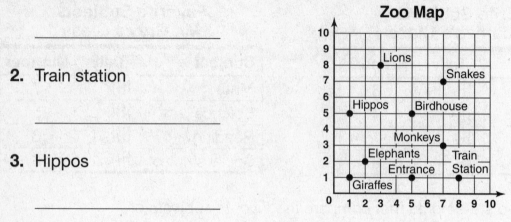

Zoo Map

Give the name of the attraction located by each ordered pair.

4. (3, 8) _____   5. (7, 3) _____

6. Which attraction is closest to the center of the grid? _____

7. The train ride begins at the train station and stops at the attractions in this order: monkeys, birdhouse, lions, hippos, and elephants. Write the ordered pairs of the train's stops in order.

Test Prep

8. Which point is at (7, 2)?

   A. *A*

   B. *B*

   C. *C*

   D. *D*

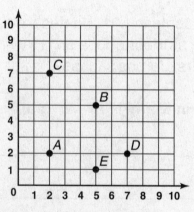

9. **Writing in Math** Cooper says the ordered pair for point *E* on the grid above is (1, 5). Do you agree? Explain.

_____

Reading Line Graphs

The students in Mr. Blake's room collected newspapers for the recycling drive.

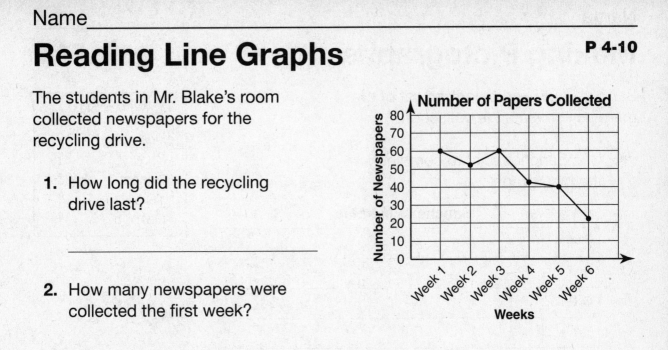

Number of Papers Collected

1. How long did the recycling drive last?

_____

2. How many newspapers were collected the first week?

_____

3. What happened to the number of newspapers after the third week?

_____

4. **Number Sense** During which weeks did the students collect more than 50 newspapers?

_____

Test Prep

5. How many more games did the Sharks win in April than in June?

   A. 1

   B. 2

   C. 3

   D. 4

Games Won by Sharks

6. **Writing in Math** How does a line graph make it easy to see changes over time?

_____

_____

Making Pictographs

Sanchez made an organized list of the
marbles in his marble collection.

My Marbles	
Blue	16
Red	24
Green	28
Yellow	14
Metallic	4

1. Use Sanchez's list to complete
the pictograph.

Sanchez's Marbles

Blue	
Red	
Green	
Yellow	
Metallic	

Key Each _____ = _____ marbles.

2. Which type of marble would you say Sanchez would consider rare? Explain.

_____

_____

Test Prep

3. Where can you look to find out what each symbol stands
for on a pictograph?

A. Title   **B.** Key   **C.** Data   **D.** Symbol

4. **Writing in Math** Pamela made
a pictograph showing students'
favorite drinks. Pamela drew
3 glasses to represent the
6 students who chose chocolate
milk. Is her pictograph right?
Explain.

Favorite Drinks

Drink	Number of Students
Chocolate milk	▯ ▯ ▯
Fruit juice	▯ ▯ ▯ ▯

Key Each ▯ = 2 students.

_____

_____

Making Bar Graphs

The table shows the number of phone calls
Mrs. Walker made during five days of fundraising.
You will be using the chart to make a bar graph.

Fundraising Calls

Day	Phone Calls
Saturday	26
Sunday	19
Monday	20
Tuesday	24
Wednesday	16

1. How many bars will be on your graph?

_____

2. Use the list to finish the bar graph that Mrs. Walker started.

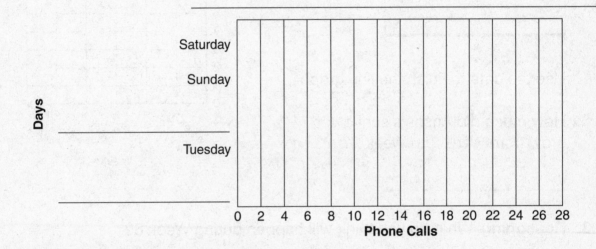

3. How many calls did Mrs. Walker make on
the weekend?

_____

Test Prep

4. Which kind of seed will be represented
by the longest bar?

Seed	Sprouts
Corn	13
Daisy	7
Marigold	5
Peas	15

   A. Corn

   B. Daisy

   C. Marigold

   D. Peas

5. Writing in Math Allen wants to compare the numbers of
tigers at different zoos. Which graph do you think he
should use, a bar graph or a line graph? Explain.

_____

Making Line Graphs

Anson kept track of how tall his sunflower was each week. His organized list is shown.

Height of Sunflower

Week	Inches
1	$\frac{1}{2}$
2	1
3	4
4	$8\frac{1}{2}$
5	13

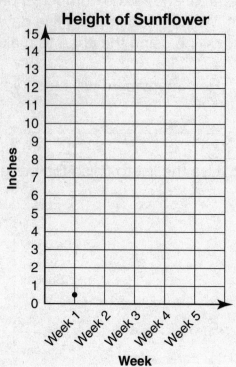

Height of Sunflower

1. Use the data to finish the line graph.

2. How much did Anson's sunflower grow from Week 2 to Week 3?

_____

3. Reasoning What do you think will happen during Week 6?

_____

_____

Test Prep

4. How many more books did Sasha read in April than in February?

A. 2   **B.** 4

C. 5   **D.** 7

5. Writing in Math Describe the difference between the number of books Sasha read in April and in May.

Number of Books Sasha Read

_____

_____

Name_____

Make a Graph

Ashley asked each person in her class
how many televisions their family owned.

Solve. Write your answer in a complete sentence.

Number of Televisions Owned

1. Complete the graph using the data .

Number of Televisions Owned
0 5 2 1 2 3 4
2 4 3 2 3 1 1
1 1 2 3 3 0 2

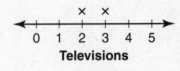

Televisions

2. Which number of televisions is most common?

_____

Devin asked his classmates each day whether or not they
made their beds that morning.

Day	Made Beds
Monday	20
Tuesday	17
Wednesday	21
Thursday	22
Friday	19

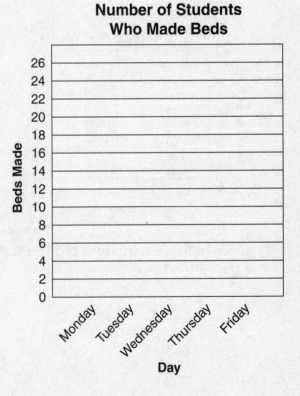

**Number of Students
Who Made Beds**

3. Complete the bar graph using the
data above.

4. On which day did Devin's classmates
make their beds the least?

_____

Car Wash

The third-grade class at Hawthorne Elementary School raised money to buy a new computer by having a car wash on the first Saturday of June.

Suppose the car wash began at 9:00 A.M. and ended at 1:00 P.M.

1. How many hours passed from the start to the finish of the car wash?   _____

2. The students took a break at 11:15 A.M. How much time passed from the start of the car wash until the break?

_____

The table shows how many cars were washed during each hour.

3. Use the table data to complete the bar graph for the number of cars washed each hour. The data for Hour 1 and Hour 3 are already completed.

Third-Grade Car Wash

Hour	Number of Cars
1	11
2	9
3	16
4	12

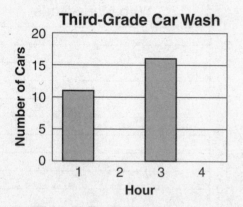

4. On which date in June did the car wash take place?

_____

June						
S	**M**	**T**	**W**	**T**	**F**	**S**
		1	2	3	4	5
6	7	8	9	10	11	12
13	14	15	16	17	18	19
20	21	22	23	24	25	26
27	28	29	30			

Multiplication as Repeated Addition   P 5-1

Complete each number sentence.

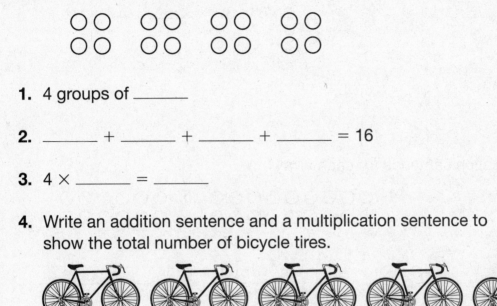

1. 4 groups of _____

2. _____ + _____ + _____ + _____ = 16

3. 4 × _____ = _____

4. Write an addition sentence and a multiplication sentence to show the total number of bicycle tires.

_____

_____

5. Number Sense Marlon has 4 baseball cards, Jake has 4 baseball cards, and Sam has 3 baseball cards. Can you write a multiplication sentence to find how many baseball cards they have altogether? Explain.

_____

_____

Test Prep

6. Which lets you put equal groups together?

A. Division   **B.** Subtraction   **C.** Estimation   **D.** Multiplication

7. Writing in Math Explain what the product of a multiplication sentence is.

_____

_____

Arrays and Multiplication

Draw an array to show each multiplication fact. Write the product.

1. $3 \times 6 =$ _____

2. $8 \times 3 =$ _____

Write a multiplication sentence for each array.

3. ○○○○○
○○○○○
○○○○○

4. ○○○○○○○○
○○○○○○○○

5. ○○○○○○
○○○○○○

_____   _____   _____

Complete. You may use counters or draw a picture to help.

6. $3 \times 7 = 21$

$7 \times$ _____ $= 21$

7. $2 \times$ _____ $= 18$

$9 \times$ _____ $= 18$

8. $4 \times 5 =$ _____

$5 \times 4 =$ _____

9. **Number Sense** Samantha says $1 + 1 + 1 = 3$ cannot be written as a multiplication sentence because there are no equal groups. Do you agree? Explain.

_____

_____

Test Prep

10. Which of the following is equal to 7×4?

A. $7 - 4$ **B.** 4×7 **C.** $4 + 7$ **D.** $7 + 4$

11. **Writing in Math** Explain how you would build arrays for both of the multiplication sentences in the above exercise.

_____

_____

Writing Multiplication Stories

Write a multiplication story for each. Draw a picture to
find each product.

1. 8 × 4

_____

_____

2. 9 × 3

_____

_____

3. Patrick works at the frozen-yogurt store after school.
Yesterday he sold 4 double-scoop strawberry cones. How
many scoops of strawberry frozen yogurt did he use?

_____

4. Fiona has 3 pet rabbits. Each rabbit eats 3 carrots a day. How
many carrots does Fiona need each day to feed her rabbits?

_____

5. **Algebra** Sara has pet spiders. She keeps all of the spiders in
the same tank. There are 24 spider legs in the tank. How many
spiders does Sara have in the tank? (Hint: a spider has 8 legs.)

_____

Test Prep

6. How many factors are in the multiplication sentence 9 × 4 = 36?

A. 1   **B.** 2   **C.** 3   **D.** 4

7. **Writing in Math** Write a multiplication story with the factors 2 and 5.

_____

_____

Name_____

Make a Table

Complete the table to solve the problem. Write the answer in a complete sentence.

1. Each centerpiece for the community banquet has 4 flowers in a vase. There needs to be 7 centerpieces. How many flowers will be used to fill the vases?

Number of vases	1	2	3	4	5	6	7
Number of flowers	4	8	12				

_____

2. Mrs. King bought 18 grapefruit at the market. Her family eats 3 grapefruit each day. How many days will the grapefruit last?

Number of grapefruit	18	15	12			
Number of days	1	2	3			

_____

3. Edmond saves $5 each week. How much will he have in his savings account at the end of 5 weeks?

Number of weeks	1	2					
Money saved	$5	$10					

_____

_____

4. **Reasoning** Will Edmond be able to buy a $36 skateboard at the end of 7 weeks? Explain.

_____

_____

Name _____

2 as a Factor

1. $2 \times 5 =$ _____   **2.** $3 \times 2 =$ _____   **3.** $2 \times \$1 =$ _____

4. $7 \times 2 =$ _____   **5.** $2 \times 9 =$ _____   **6.** $2 \times \$8 =$ _____

7. $\begin{array}{r} 4 \\ \times\ 2 \\ \hline \end{array}$ **8.** $\begin{array}{r} \$6 \\ \times\ 2 \\ \hline \end{array}$ **9.** $\begin{array}{r} 2 \\ \times\ 8 \\ \hline \end{array}$ **10.** $\begin{array}{r} 2 \\ \times\ 2 \\ \hline \end{array}$ **11.** $\begin{array}{r} 5 \\ \times\ 2 \\ \hline \end{array}$

12. Find 2 times 9. _____   **13.** Multiply 2 and 3. _____

14. Number Sense How can adding doubles help you multiply by 2?

_____

_____

_____

15. Algebra Write two multiplication sentences that have 2 as
a factor and a product of 12.

_____

16. Mrs. Freedon walks 2 mi each day. How many
miles will she walk in 1 week?   _____

17. How many miles will Mrs. Freedon walk in 2 weeks?   _____

Test Prep

18. Which number is a multiple of 2?

A. 15   **B.** 17   **C.** 21   **D.** 32

19. Writing in Math Madison has 7 pairs of shoes in her closet. Write
a multiplication sentence to show how many shoes Madison has.
Then solve the problem. Write your answer in a complete sentence.

_____

_____

Name _____

5 as a Factor

1. $4 \times 5 =$ _____   2. $\$9 \times 5 =$ _____   3. $5 \times 7 =$ _____

4. $3 \times 5 =$ _____   5. $5 \times 2 =$ _____   6. $\$5 \times 5 =$ _____

7.   8   8.   1   9.   5   10.   5   11.   5
   $\times \$5$ $\times 5$ $\times 6$ $\times 5$ $\times 3$

12. **Number Sense** What are two ways to skip count to find 2×5?

_____

13. **Algebra** Write a number sentence to show
    that 5 is a factor of 35.   _____

14. There are 5 days in each school week. On how
    many days will you attend school over 9 weeks?   _____

15. Seth has 45 pennies. Draw an array that shows how many
    nickels the pennies are worth.

Test Prep

16. Jay's favorite restaurant has 8 tables. Each table can seat
    5 people. How many people can the restaurant seat?

    A. 13 people   **B.** 40 people   **C.** 45 people   **D.** 58 people

17. **Writing in Math** Is 115 a multiple of 5? Tell how you know.

_____

_____

10 as a Factor

1. $0 \times 10 =$ _____   **2.** $10 \times 9 =$ _____   **3.** $2 \times \$10 =$ _____

4. $6 \times 10 =$ _____   **5.** $10 \times 1 =$ _____   **6.** $10 \times \$3 =$ _____

7.	**8.**	**9.**	**10.**	**11.**
$\begin{array}{r} 10 \\ \times\ \$8 \\ \hline \end{array}$	$\begin{array}{r} 10 \\ \times\ 4 \\ \hline \end{array}$	$\begin{array}{r} 10 \\ \times\ 7 \\ \hline \end{array}$	$\begin{array}{r} 10 \\ \times\ 3 \\ \hline \end{array}$	$\begin{array}{r} 10 \\ \times\ 2 \\ \hline \end{array}$

12. Reasoning How can counting by 10s help you multiply by 10s?

_____

_____

_____

13. Mary Ann earns $10 each week walking the neighborhood dogs. How much will she earn in 7 weeks?

_____

14. How long will it take Mary Ann to save $150?

_____

15. Number Sense Draw 3 arrays to show that 20 is a multiple of 2, 5, and 10.

Test Prep

16. Which is NOT a multiple of 10?

A. 30   **B.** 80   **C.** 100   **D.** 101

17. Writing in Math How can multiples of 10 also be multiples of 5?

_____

Multiple-Step Problems

Write and answer the hidden question or questions. Then solve the problem.

1. Dave swam 6 laps and did 9 dives at the swimming pool. Crystal did 4 dives and swam 8 laps. How many more laps than dives did Crystal and Dave do?

_____

_____

_____

For 2–5, use the cookbook.

2. Polly has 8 strawberries, 1 c milk, and 10 ice cubes. She makes a strawberry smoothie. What ingredients does she have left?

_____

_____

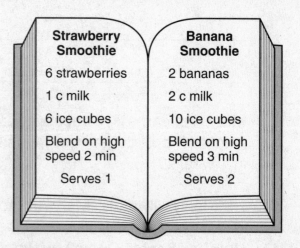

Strawberry Smoothie	Banana Smoothie
6 strawberries	2 bananas
1 c milk	2 c milk
6 ice cubes	10 ice cubes
Blend on high speed 2 min	Blend on high speed 3 min
Serves 1	Serves 2

3. Matt wants to make both recipes. He has 2 dozen ice cubes. Does he have enough ice cubes? Explain.

_____

_____

4. Julian wants to make banana smoothies for himself and 3 of his friends. How many bananas will he need?

_____

_____

5. **Writing in Math** Use the smoothie recipes to write a word problem with a hidden question. Then solve the problem.

_____

_____

Multiplying with 0 and 1

1. $1 \times 4 =$ _____   **2.** $3 \times 0 =$ _____   **3.** $\$9 \times 1 =$ _____

4. $0 \times 1 =$ _____   **5.** $2 \times 0 =$ _____   **6.** $0 \times 9 =$ _____

7. $\begin{array}{r} 5 \\ \times\, 1 \\ \hline \end{array}$ **8.** $\begin{array}{r} 1 \\ \times\, 7 \\ \hline \end{array}$ **9.** $\begin{array}{r} 10 \\ \times\, 0 \\ \hline \end{array}$ **10.** $\begin{array}{r} 6 \\ \times\, \$1 \\ \hline \end{array}$ **11.** $\begin{array}{r} 1 \\ \times\, 8 \\ \hline \end{array}$

Compare. Write $<$, $>$, or $=$ for each _____.

12. 1×5 _____ 7×0 **13.** 0×17 _____ 38×0

14. 1×97 _____ 97×1 **15.** 0×51 _____ 1×51

Write $\times$ or $+$ for each _____.

16. 1 _____ $7 = 7$ **17.** 8 _____ $0 = 8$

18. 9 _____ $1 = 10$ **19.** 3 _____ $0 = 0$

20. Sara keeps 4 boxes under her bed. Each box is for holding a different type of seashell. There are 0 shells in each box. Write a multiplication sentence to show how many seashells Sara has.

_____

Test Prep

21. Which is the product of 6×1?

   A. 7   **B.** 6   **C.** 5   **D.** 1

22. **Writing in Math** Angela says that the product of 0×0 is the same as the sum of $0 + 0$. Do you agree? Explain.

_____

_____

Name _____

9 as a Factor

1. $9 \times 4 =$ _____   **2.** $7 \times 9 =$ _____   **3.** $\$9 \times 9 =$ _____

4. $0 \times 9 =$ _____   **5.** $9 \times 3 =$ _____   **6.** $9 \times 2 =$ _____

7. $\begin{array}{r} 9 \\ \times\ 5 \\ \hline \end{array}$ **8.** $\begin{array}{r} 10 \\ \times\ 9 \\ \hline \end{array}$ **9.** $\begin{array}{r} \$2 \\ \times\ 9 \\ \hline \end{array}$ **10.** $\begin{array}{r} 9 \\ \times\ 6 \\ \hline \end{array}$ **11.** $\begin{array}{r} 9 \\ \times\ 1 \\ \hline \end{array}$

12. Multiply 4 and 9. _____   **13.** Find 3 times 9. _____

14. Paula's mother put Paula's hair into 9 braids.
Each braid used 3 beads. How many beads
did Paula's mother use?   _____

15. Number the fingers to help multiply 5×9.
Cross out the finger you could bend
down to show 5×9. Find 5×9.

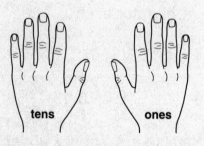

tens   ones

_____

16. **Number Sense** Explain how the finger
pattern helped you find 5×9.

_____

_____

_____

Test Prep

17. $2 + 2 + 2 + 2 + 2 + 2 + 2 + 2 + 2 =$ _____

   A. 2×9 **B.** $2 + 9$ **C.** 9×9 **D.** $9 - 2$

18. **Writing in Math** Write a multiplication story for 9×8.

_____

_____

Practicing Multiplication Facts

1. $9 \times 8 =$ _____   **2.** $5 \times 4 =$ _____   **3.** $1 \times 2 =$ _____

4. $7 \times 0 =$ _____   **5.** $8 \times 10 =$ _____   **6.** $6 \times 2 =$ _____

7. $\begin{array}{r} 5 \\ \times\ 6 \\ \hline \end{array}$ **8.** $\begin{array}{r} 3 \\ \times\ 5 \\ \hline \end{array}$ **9.** $\begin{array}{r} 9 \\ \times\ 4 \\ \hline \end{array}$ **10.** $\begin{array}{r} 1 \\ \times\ 1 \\ \hline \end{array}$ **11.** $\begin{array}{r} 2 \\ \times\ 7 \\ \hline \end{array}$

Algebra Write the missing numbers.

12. $7 \times$ _____ $= 0$ **13.** _____ $\times 4 = 36$

14. $2 \times$ _____ $= 4$ **15.** $8 \times$ _____ $= 40$

16. Number Sense Is 30 a multiple of 5? How do you know?

_____

_____

17. Seven friends went to the carnival. Each spent $0.20 on tickets. How much did they spend altogether on the tickets?   _____

Test Prep

18. Which is the product of 1×0?

A. 9×9 **B.** 0×9 **C.** 9×1 **D.** 1×9

19. Writing in Math Stacy multiplied 5×9 and said the answer was 44. What two patterns could you use to show that her answer is not correct?

_____

_____

_____

Name_____

Measure Your Lunch

Liquid and dry measurements use either customary units or metric units. If you go to a supermarket today or simply look in the kitchen, you will see that many of the products your family buys have both customary units and metric unit information.

1. A small can of soup weighs about 10 oz. Write an addition sentence and a multiplication sentence for about how many ounces of soup there are in 7 cans.

   _____

   _____

2. One serving of chicken-with-rice soup contains 8 g of carbohydrates. How many grams of carbohydrates are there in 5 servings of the soup?   _____

3. One can of condensed chicken-with-rice soup contains 5 g of protein. Finish the table to find the total amount of protein in different numbers of cans.

Number of cans	1	2								
Grams of protein	5	10								

4. A small container of mixed-berry yogurt has 10 mg of cholesterol. How many milligrams of cholesterol are there in 4 small containers of mixed-berry yogurt?

   _____

5. A small container of mixed-berry yogurt also has 9 g of protein. The recommended daily allowance of protein is about 45 grams. About how many small containers of mixed-berry yogurt do you have to eat to get the recommended daily amount of protein?

   _____

Name_____

3 as a Factor

1. $1 \times 3 =$ _____   2. $3 \times 7 =$ _____   3. $\$6 \times 3 =$ _____

4. $8 \times 3 =$ _____   5. $3 \times 8 =$ _____   6. $3 \times 5 =$ _____

7.	8.	9.	10.	11.
$\begin{array}{r} 3 \\ \times\, 2 \\ \hline \end{array}$	$\begin{array}{r} 4 \\ \times\, 3 \\ \hline \end{array}$	$\begin{array}{r} 3 \\ \times\, 0 \\ \hline \end{array}$	$\begin{array}{r} \$3 \\ \times\, 5 \\ \hline \end{array}$	$\begin{array}{r} 3 \\ \times\, 9 \\ \hline \end{array}$

12. **Number Sense** What two multiplication facts can be added to find 3×7?

_____

13. There were 5 people who bought tickets to a football game. They each bought 3 tickets. How many tickets were bought altogether?   _____

14. Marina has 3 colors of flowers. She has 3 of each color. How many flowers does she have altogether?   _____

15. A group of 7 friends paid $3 each to get into a carnival. How much did they pay altogether?   _____

Test Prep

16. Tom gave each of his 5 friends 3 stickers. How many stickers did he give away?

   A. 3 stickers   **B.** 5 stickers   **C.** 12 stickers   **D.** 15 stickers

17. **Writing in Math** Explain how you can break apart 3×9 to help you multiply.

_____

_____

_____

Name_____

4 as a Factor

1. $2 \times 4 =$ _____   **2.** $4 \times 5 =$ _____   **3.** $3 \times 4 =$ _____

4. $4 \times 4 =$ _____   **5.** $\$4 \times 8 =$ _____   **6.** $4 \times 6 =$ _____

7.   1   **8.**   4   **9.** $4   **10.**   0   **11.**   4
     $\underline{\times\ 4}$ $\underline{\times\ 4}$ $\underline{\times\ 9}$ $\underline{\times\ 4}$ $\underline{\times\ 7}$

12. **Number Sense** What multiplication fact can
you double to find 4×7?   _____

13. Continue each pattern.

   a. 20, 16, 12, _____, _____, _____

   b. 20, 24, 28, _____, _____, _____

   c. 8, 12, 16, _____, _____, _____

14. There are 6 chairs around a table. Each chair
has 4 legs. How many chair legs are around
the table?   _____

15. Sally bought 4 movie tickets for herself and her
friends. The tickets cost $8 each. How much
money did Sally spend on the movie tickets?   _____

Test Prep

16. Aaron changed the tires on 5 cars. Each car had 4 tires.
How many tires did Aaron change?

   A. 12 tires   **B.** 16 tires   **C.** 20 tires   **D.** 24 tires

17. **Writing in Math** Tessie multiplied 3×4, and then doubled
it to find 6×8. Did she get the correct answer? Explain.

_____

_____

Name _____

6 and 7 as Factors

1. $5 \times 6 =$ _____
2. $6 \times 3 =$ _____
3. $6 \times 8 =$ _____

4. $\$3 \times 7 =$ _____
5. $7 \times 10 =$ _____
6. $7 \times 4 =$ _____

7. $\begin{array}{r} \$4 \\ \times\ 6 \\ \hline \end{array}$
8. $\begin{array}{r} 5 \\ \times\ 7 \\ \hline \end{array}$
9. $\begin{array}{r} 7 \\ \times\ 8 \\ \hline \end{array}$
10. $\begin{array}{r} 6 \\ \times\ 6 \\ \hline \end{array}$
11. $\begin{array}{r} 6 \\ \times\ 7 \\ \hline \end{array}$

12. Multiply 7 and 7. _____
13. Multiply 1 and 6. _____

14. Find the product of 6 and 9. _____
15. Find 7 times 2. _____

16. **Number Sense** What multiplication fact can be found by using the arrays for 2×9 and 5×9? _____

17. Raul's science class is hatching chicken eggs. If the eggs take 3 weeks to hatch, how many days until they hatch? _____

18. Emily cut 7 apples into slices. There are 6 slices from each apple. How many apple slices did she cut in all? _____

Test Prep

19. Helen needs 6 more stuffed miniature bears to complete her collection. Each bear costs $9. How much will Helen have to spend to complete her collection?

A. $45   **B.** $54   **C.** $56   **D.** $63

20. **Writing in Math** Explain how you could use $5 \times 6 = 30$ to find the product of 6×6.

_____

_____

_____

Name_____

8 as a Factor

1. $1 \times 8 = $ _____

2. $8 \times 0 = $ _____

3. $\$8 \times 3 = $ _____

4. $2 \times 8 = $ _____

5. $8 \times 7 = $ _____

6. $8 \times 6 = $ _____

7. $\$3$
      $\underline{\times\ 8}$

8. 8
      $\underline{\times\ 1}$

9. 4
      $\underline{\times\ 8}$

10. 8
       $\underline{\times\ 9}$

11. 8
       $\underline{\times\ 5}$

12. An octopus has 8 arms. At the zoo, there were
3 octopuses in one tank. How many arms were
in the tank altogether?   _____

13. For every hour Carrie works at the restaurant,
she earns $8. She worked 7 hr yesterday.
How much did she earn?   _____

Test Prep

14. Each package of cheese contains 10 slices. Each package
of rolls contains 8 rolls. Ted bought 5 packages of each.
How many rolls did he buy?

A. 35 rolls   **B.** 40 rolls   **C.** 50 rolls   **D.** 80 rolls

15. Writing in Math Carlos used two arrays
to find 8×6. Fix Carlos's error and then
give the correct answer.   _____

○ ○ ○   ○ ○ ○
○ ○ ○   ○ ○ ○
○ ○ ○   ○ ○ ○
○ ○ ○   ○ ○ ○

Practicing Multiplication Facts

1. $8 \times 3 =$ _____   **2.** $4 \times 7 =$ _____   **3.** $6 \times 8 =$ _____

4. $5 \times 9 =$ _____   **5.** $7 \times 8 =$ _____   **6.** $5 \times 7 =$ _____

7. $\begin{array}{r} 6 \\ \times\ 2 \\ \hline \end{array}$ **8.** $\begin{array}{r} 4 \\ \times\ 6 \\ \hline \end{array}$ **9.** $\begin{array}{r} 10 \\ \times\ 0 \\ \hline \end{array}$ **10.** $\begin{array}{r} 3 \\ \times\ 5 \\ \hline \end{array}$ **11.** $\begin{array}{r} 4 \\ \times\ 9 \\ \hline \end{array}$

12. Number Sense How can you use the multiplication facts
for 3 to help you find the multiplication facts for 9?

_____

_____

13. Lee puts 4 napkins on each tray. Complete the table.

Trays	1	2	3	4	5
Napkins	4				

14. How many napkins will Lee have on 10 trays? _____

Test Prep

15. Linda gets $6 for each dog that she walks. Yesterday she
walked 5 dogs, and today she walked 2 dogs. How much
did Linda make in two days for walking the dogs?

A. $12   **B.** $30   **C.** $42   **D.** $48

16. Writing in Math Explain another way to help you find the
product of 8×6 without using repeated addition.

_____

_____

_____

PROBLEM-SOLVING STRATEGY

Look for a Pattern

Describe patterns you see. Write the answer in a complete sentence.

1. Dillon is making a necklace with black and white beads. Which colors will be used for the next 3 beads?

_____

_____

_____

2. Nancy is making a pattern using circles. How many circles will she draw for the next design in the pattern?

_____

_____

_____

3. Alisha was walking on a sidewalk and noticed the pattern below in the color of the blocks. She walked over 27 blocks that were in the pattern. How many darker blocks did she walk over?

_____

4. **Writing in Math** Linda has 18 quarters, 12 dimes, and 7 pennies. She wants to make a pattern of quarter, quarter, penny, dime, and quarter. How many of these patterns can she make? Explain.

_____

_____

Using Multiplication to Compare

1. Jim has lost 3 times as many teeth as his brother Justin. Justin has lost 3 teeth. How many teeth has Jim lost?

Teeth Justin Lost	3
Teeth Jim Lost	

_____

2. Sarah has 6 seashells. She has 7 times as many pieces of beach glass as she does seashells. How many pieces of beach glass does she have? _____

3. The hardware store stocks 3 times as many gallons of white paint as they do gallons of gray paint. How many gallons of white paint are kept in stock at the hardware store?

Painting Supplies

Item	Number
Large paintbrush	12
Small paintbrush	18
Black paint	3
Gray paint	6
Green paint	4
Red paint	6
White paint	

_____

4. **Number Sense** Tom has $8. Becky has 4 times as many dollars as Tom. How much money do they have altogether?

_____

Test Prep

5. Gina's house has 9 windows. Jonathan's house has twice as many windows as Gina's. How many windows are in Jonathan's house?

A. 9 windows   **B.** 18 windows   **C.** 21 windows   **D.** 27 windows

6. **Writing in Math** Katie picked 7 times as many strawberries as Garrett. Garrett picked 6 quarts of strawberries. How many quarts did Katie pick? Which two multiplication facts can you use to help find the solution?

_____

_____

Patterns on a Table

1. $3 \times 9 =$ _____ **2.** $11 \times 10 =$ _____ **3.** $5 \times 7 =$ _____

4. $8 \times 7 =$ _____ **5.** $12 \times 4 =$ _____ **6.** $11 \times 5 =$ _____

7. $\begin{array}{r} 12 \\ \times\ 6 \\ \hline \end{array}$ **8.** $\begin{array}{r} 11 \\ \times\ 12 \\ \hline \end{array}$ **9.** $\begin{array}{r} 9 \\ \times\ 7 \\ \hline \end{array}$ **10.** $\begin{array}{r} 3 \\ \times\ 8 \\ \hline \end{array}$ **11.** $\begin{array}{r} 12 \\ \times\ 4 \\ \hline \end{array}$

12. Number Sense Could there be a number in the 2s column on the multiplication table that ends in a 5? Explain why or why not.

_____

_____

_____

13. A mouse eats about 11 calories each day. About how many calories does it eat in 8 days? _____

Test Prep

14. George and Shelley filled egg cartons with decorated eggs. A dozen eggs fits into each carton. They filled 6 cartons. How many decorated eggs did they have?

A. 54 eggs **B.** 60 eggs **C.** 66 eggs **D.** 72 eggs

15. Writing in Math Explain how you could use a 10s fact to find a 9s fact.

_____

_____

_____

Multiplying with Three Factors

1. $1 \times 2 \times 3 =$ _____   **2.** $2 \times 2 \times 4 =$ _____   **3.** $8 \times 2 \times 2 =$ _____

4. $6 \times 2 \times 1 =$ _____   **5.** $5 \times 5 \times 2 =$ _____   **6.** $3 \times 3 \times 3 =$ _____

7. $1 \times 7 \times 8 =$ _____   **8.** $0 \times 9 \times 8 =$ _____   **9.** $6 \times 2 \times 5 =$ _____

10. Number Sense Harvey says $9 \times 8 \times$ (any other number)
will always be greater than the product of $2 \times 9 \times 4$.
Do you agree? Explain.

_____

_____

_____

11. Write three ways to find $3 \times 2 \times 4$.

_____

12. Sarah and Amanda each have 2 bags with
4 marbles in each. How many marbles do
they have altogether?   _____

13. Jesse bought 2 sheets of stamps. On each
sheet there are 5 rows of stamps with 6 stamps
in each row. How many stamps did Jesse buy?   _____

Test Prep

14. Which is the product of $2 \times 3 \times 2$?

A. 6   **B.** 7   **C.** 10   **D.** 12

15. Writing in Math A classroom has 6 tables. The teacher
puts 2 pencils, 1 eraser, and 1 sheet of stickers into each
bag, and puts 4 bags on each table. How many pencils
did the teacher put in the bags altogether? Write a
multiplication sentence and solve the problem.

_____

Find a Rule

Write a rule for each table. Complete the table.

1.

Number of boxes	1	2	3	4	5
Number of grapefruits	4	8			

2.

Number of people	1	2	3	4	5
Number of fingers	10	20			

3.

In	6	2	7	1	4
Out	18	6	21		

4. Number Sense Caleb filled baskets with flowers. He filled 5 baskets with the same number of roses in each basket. He used 35 roses. How many roses went into each basket? _____

Test Prep

5. The rule for a table is *Multiply by 5*. If a 3 is the **In** number, what is the **Out** number?

A. 15 **B.** 10 **C.** 5 **D.** 3

6. Writing in Math What is the multiplication rule for this table? Why doesn't the rule *Add 6* work? Complete the table.

In	6	7	8	9	10
Out	12				20

Choose an Operation

Draw a picture to show the main idea. Then choose an operation and solve the problem.

Sam joined a movie club that gives 4 points for every DVD movie. Sam can use his points to get the items on the flyer.

1. Sam has bought 7 DVD movies so far.
   How many points has he earned?

2. Sam exchanges some of his points for the movie passes.
   How many points does he have left?

3. Sam wants the baseball cap. He can use the points he has left. How many more points does Sam need to get the cap? How many more DVD movies will he need to buy?

PROBLEM-SOLVING APPLICATIONS
Television

In 2002, there were 10 national and international stations. There were also 56 national cable-program channels. A newspaper lists the TV-programming schedule each day for evening viewing from 8:00 P.M. until 12:30 A.M.

1. During that time period, 8 cable stations will show 2 movies each. How many movies will be shown then? _____

2. During that same period, 6 other cable stations will show 3 movies each. How many movies will be shown by those 6 cable stations? _____

3. From 8:00 P.M. to 12:30 A.M., 6 of the network channels will each have a total of 5 programs. How many programs will be shown by those channels? _____

4. There are 4 cable channels that will show nine 30-minute programs during this period. How many programs will be shown by those 4 cable channels? _____

5. Between 8:00 P.M. and 12:30 A.M., Network A shows 7 programs, Network B shows 6 programs, Network C shows 5 programs, and Network D shows 9 programs. Which networks show more programs altogether, Networks A and B, or Networks C and D? Explain.

_____

_____

A newspaper costs $0.50 an issue. Suppose you bought the newspaper using only one type of coin, either dimes, nickels, or pennies.

6. How many dimes would you need to buy a newspaper? _____

7. How many nickels would you need? _____

8. How many pennies would you need? _____

Division as Sharing

Use counters or draw a picture to solve.

1. 3 bicycles   6 wheels

   How many wheels are on each bicycle?   _____

2. 12 tennis balls   4 canisters

   How many tennis balls are in each canister?   _____

3. 16 bananas   4 bunches

   How many bananas are in each bunch?   _____

4. **Number Sense** One box contains
   12 granola bars. Two bars are in each
   package. How many packages are in
   each box of granola bars?   _____

5. Isabella and her 5 friends went to a concert
   at the school. They spent a total of $42
   for the tickets. Each ticket was the same
   price. How much was each ticket?   _____

6. In a yearbook club, a teacher gave out 3 new
   folders to each student. The teacher gave out
   27 folders in all. How many students are in
   the yearbook club?   _____

Test Prep

7. Which is the quotient of 20 ÷ 5?

   A. 2   **B.** 3   **C.** 4   **D.** 5

8. **Writing in Math** Tanya and her family went out for frozen
   yogurt. They ordered 10 scoops of frozen yogurt. Every
   person received 2 scoops. Explain how to find the number
   of people in Tanya's family. Then write the answer.

   _____

Division as Repeated Subtraction

Use counters or draw a picture to solve.

1. 35 stickers

5 stickers on each sheet

How many sheets?

_____

2. 40 leaves

4 leaves painted on each vase

How many vases?

On Mackinac Island in Michigan, people rent bicycles because no cars are allowed on the island. The table shows the number of people who rode tandem bicycles each month. Two people ride on each tandem bicycle. How many bicycles were rented each month?

People Renting Tandem Bicycles

Month	People
May	8
June	24
July	16
August	22
September	14

3. May _____

4. June _____

5. July _____

6. August _____

7. How many bicycles were rented in all? _____

Test Prep

8. Keisha has to carry 24 boxes to her room. She can carry 3 boxes on each trip. How many trips will she take?

A. 7 trips   **B.** 8 trips   **C.** 9 trips   **D.** 10 trips

9. Writing in Math Tamara says that $15 \div 3 = 5$. Is she correct? Explain how you know.

_____

_____

Writing Division Stories

Write a division story for each number sentence.
Then use counters or draw a picture to solve.

1. $54 \div 6 = \square$

2. $36 \div 9 = x$

_____

_____

_____

In Colonial times, people held quilting bees. During a quilting bee, people would get together and work to make quilts. Suppose each person brought the same number of pieces of cloth to make the quilt.

Size of Quilt

	Twin	Full	Queen
Pieces of Cloth	50	77	108

3. If 10 people come to the quilting bee, how many pieces would each person need to bring to make a twin-size quilt? _____

4. What size quilt can the people make if 9 people each bring 12 pieces of cloth? _____

Test Prep

5. If you have 21 ice cubes, and 7 ice cubes are in each cup of juice, how many cups do you need?

A. 2 cups   **B.** 3 cups   **C.** 4 cups   **D.** 5 cups

6. Writing in Math Copy and finish the story shown for $22 \div 2$. Use counters or draw a picture to find the answer. Then write your own division story for $22 \div 2$.

Justin has 22 ■. He wants to put 2 ■ in each group. How many groups will there be?

_____

_____

PROBLEM-SOLVING STRATEGY

Try, Check, and Revise

Solve. Write each answer in a sentence.

1. Olivia has 16 slices of bread and 2 rolls. How many sandwiches can she make?

   _____

2. Benjamin has 18 video games and 4 board games. He buys two new video games. How many games does he have in all?

   _____

3. Savannah is making a flower arrangement. She can choose 12 roses. She can choose equal amounts of 4 different colors. How many of each color can she choose?

   _____

4. Christian went fishing today for 2 hr. He caught 3 fish in the first hour he was fishing. He caught the same number of fish the second hour. He caught 2 more fish yesterday than he caught today. How many fish did he catch yesterday?

   _____

5. Four lines are drawn on a piece of paper. The third line is blue. The line above the blue line is red. The fourth line is orange. The first line is yellow. What color is the second line?

   _____

6. **Writing in Math** Ms. Ricardo has 21 students in her class. She has 5 tables in the classroom. If all of the students sit at the tables, will there be an equal number of students at each table? Explain.

   _____

   _____

Relating Multiplication and Division

Complete. Use counters or draw a picture to help.

1. $4 \times$ _____ $= 20$

$20 \div 4 =$ _____

2. $8 \times$ _____ $= 56$

$56 \div 8 =$ _____

3. $9 \times$ _____ $= 72$

$72 \div 9 =$ _____

4. $7 \times$ _____ $= 42$

$42 \div 7 =$ _____

5. $6 \times$ _____ $= 54$

$54 \div 6 =$ _____

6. $2 \times$ _____ $= 10$

$10 \div 2 =$ _____

7. Number Sense Write a fact family for 3, 6, and 18.

_____

_____

8. Patrick purchased 8 books at the resale shop. He needed 4 books for each of his projects at school. How many projects did he have?   _____

Test Prep

9. A copy store charges $10 for 100 copies on white paper and $15 for 100 copies on colored paper. Kaylee paid $40 for 300 copies. How many copies were on colored paper?

A. 100 copies   **B.** 200 copies   **C.** 300 copies   **D.** 500 copies

10. Writing in Math Evan told his class that the people in his family have 14 legs altogether. Quinton said Evan must have 7 people in his family. Is Quinton correct? Explain why or why not.

_____

_____

Name_____

Dividing with 2 and 5

1. $20 \div 5 =$ _____   2. $16 \div 2 =$ _____   3. $12 \div 2 =$ _____

4. $40 \div 5 =$ _____   5. $25 \div 5 =$ _____   6. $8 \div 2 =$ _____

7. $30 \div 5 =$ _____   8. $10 \div 2 =$ _____   9. $15 \div 5 =$ _____

10. Find $45 \div 5.$ _____   11. Divide 14 by 2. _____

12. **Number Sense** Explain how you can use multiplication to help you find $20 \div 5$.

_____

_____

13. A wolf spider has 8 eyes and 8 legs. How many spiders would there be if there were 16 eyes and 16 legs?   _____

14. William has 1 quarter, 2 dimes, and 1 nickel. Abigail has $0.10 more than William and has only nickels. How many nickels does Abigail have?   _____

15. Gabriella and 4 friends shared a pack of 15 gluesticks equally. How many gluesticks did each person get?   _____

Test Prep

16. John has 25 colored pencils. If John equally divides the pencils between 5 people, how many pencils will each person get?

    A. 2 pencils   **B.** 4 pencils   **C.** 5 pencils   **D.** 7 pencils

17. **Writing in Math** Franklin says that if he divides 50 by 5, he will get 10. Jeff says he should get 9. Who is correct? Explain.

_____

_____

Dividing with 3 and 4

1. $9 \div 3 =$ _____   **2.** $40 \div 4 =$ _____   **3.** $21 \div 3 =$ _____

4. $32 \div 4 =$ _____   **5.** $30 \div 3 =$ _____   **6.** $18 \div 3 =$ _____

7. $20 \div 4 =$ _____   **8.** $24 \div 3 =$ _____   **9.** $36 \div 4 =$ _____

10. $4\overline{)28}$ **11.** $3\overline{)15}$ **12.** $4\overline{)16}$

13. Divide 27 by 3. _____   **14.** Find 32 divided by 4. _____

15. Number Sense Explain how you can use $4 \times 5 = 20$ to find $20 \div 4$.

_____

_____

16. The third-grade class is making a display for
science. The poster board they are using is 36 in.
long. The teacher needs to cut it into 3 equal
pieces. How long will each piece be?   _____

Test Prep

17. Which is the quotient of $40 \div 4$?

A. 7   **B.** 8   **C.** 9   **D.** 10

18. Writing in Math Wendell has a box with 32 cherries. He
shares the cherries equally with 3 friends. Bonnie received
7 cherries. She thinks she should have one more. Is she
correct? Explain.

_____

_____

_____

Dividing with 6 and 7

1. $36 \div 6 =$ _____
2. $42 \div 6 =$ _____
3. $70 \div 7 =$ _____

4. $60 \div 6 =$ _____
5. $56 \div 7 =$ _____
6. $49 \div 7 =$ _____

7. $6 \div 6 =$ _____
8. $28 \div 7 =$ _____
9. $18 \div 6 =$ _____

10. $6\overline{)24}$
11. $7\overline{)35}$
12. $6\overline{)30}$

13. Divide 12 by 6. _____

14. Find 42 divided by 7. _____

15. **Number Sense** How many groups of 6 are there in 36?
Explain how you know.

_____

_____

16. Connor has 48 apples. He separated the
apples equally into 6 crates. How many
apples are there in each crate?   _____

17. Sierra's karate class lasts 56 days. How
many weeks does the class last?   _____

Test Prep

18. Jada's third-grade class is leaving on a field trip. There are
32 people going on the field trip. The group will ride in vans
that each hold 8 people. How many vans will the class need?

   A. 4 vans   **B.** 5 vans   **C.** 6 vans   **D.** 7 vans

19. **Writing in Math** Kyle says there are exactly 4 weeks in
February. Is he right? Explain.

_____

_____

Dividing with 8 and 9

1. 27 ÷ 9 = _____   **2.** 45 ÷ 9 = _____   **3.** 72 ÷ 8 = _____

4. 81 ÷ 9 = _____   **5.** 24 ÷ 8 = _____   **6.** 63 ÷ 9 = _____

7. 64 ÷ 8 = _____   **8.** 36 ÷ 9 = _____   **9.** 48 ÷ 8 = _____

10. 9)18   **11.** 8)40   **12.** 9)72

13. Find 16 divided by 8. _____   **14.** Divide 90 by 9. _____

15. Number Sense What multiplication fact can help you find 32 ÷ 8?

_____

_____

16. Nicholas scored 16 runs in the first 8 baseball games
he played. If he scored the same number of times in
each game, how many runs did he score in each game? _____

Test Prep

17. Mr. Carlos brought 32 pencils to school. He shared them
equally among the 8 students in the math group. How
many pencils did each student get?

A. 2 pencils   **B.** 3 pencils   **C.** 4 pencils   **D.** 5 pencils

18. Writing in Math Adam made 19 paper cranes on Monday
and 8 on Tuesday. He gave 9 of his friends an equal
number of cranes. How many did each friend receive?
Explain how you found your answer.

_____

_____

Name_____

Dividing with 0 and 1

1. $9 \div 1 =$ _____

2. $0 \div 8 =$ _____

3. $7 \div 7 =$ _____

4. $0 \div 9 =$ _____

5. $3 \div 3 =$ _____

6. $6 \div 1 =$ _____

7. $1\overline{)3}$

8. $4\overline{)4}$

9. $8\overline{)0}$

10. Divide 0 by 2. _____

11. Divide 7 by 1. _____

12. **Number Sense** Explain how you know that $45 \div 0$ cannot be done.

_____

_____

Compare. Use $<$, $>$, or $=$.

13. $6 \div 6$ $\bigcirc$ $4 \div 4$

14. $0 \div 5$ $\bigcirc$ $5 \div 5$

15. $10 \div 1$ $\bigcirc$ $7 \div 1$

Test Prep

16. Which is the quotient of $0 \div 9$?

A. 9

B. 5

C. 1

D. 0

17. **Writing in Math** Explain why $10 - 0 = 10$ but $0 \div 10 = 0$.

_____

_____

_____

_____

Remainders

Use counters or draw a picture to find each quotient and remainder.

1. $39 \div 6 =$ _____   **2.** $20 \div 3 =$ _____   **3.** $11 \div 3 =$ _____

4. $9 \div 2 =$ _____   **5.** $7 \div 3 =$ _____   **6.** $13 \div 6 =$ _____

7. $36 \div 3 =$ _____   **8.** $25 \div 4 =$ _____   **9.** $45 \div 6 =$ _____

10. Holly bought a box of 65 souvenir magnets on her vacation. She wants to share them equally with her 9 friends. How many magnets will each friend get? How many magnets will be left over?

_____

11. Sebastian and Caitlin have 11 thank-you cards to send. They agreed that if each of them sends 5 they will be finished. Do you agree? Explain.

_____

Test Prep

12. Yvonne can carry 7 books at one time, and she wants to carry 25 books to her room. How many books will she carry on her fourth trip?

A. 1 book   **B.** 2 books   **C.** 3 books   **D.** 4 books

13. Writing in Math Anna has 30 fruit snacks that she wants to share with her class. Because there are 25 people in her class, Anna used $30 \div 25$ to find the number of snacks she will have left over. Will she find the correct answer? Explain.

_____

_____

Division Patterns with 10, 11, and 12 P 7-12

Find each quotient. You may use a multiplication table,
counters, or draw a picture to help.

1. $121 \div 11 =$ _____   **2.** $70 \div 7 =$ _____   **3.** $132 \div 11 =$ _____

4. $72 \div 12 =$ _____   **5.** $66 \div 6 =$ _____   **6.** $40 \div 4 =$ _____

7. $300 \div 30 =$ _____   **8.** $22 \div 2 =$ _____   **9.** $200 \div 10 =$ _____

10. $8\overline{)88}$ **11.** $9\overline{)36}$ **12.** $10\overline{)110}$

13. Number Sense Adrian said that any 2-digit number with
2 identical digits is divisible by 11. Do you agree? Explain.

_____

_____

14. Madeline purchased 10 sweaters for $100.
How much did she spend for each sweater?   _____

Test Prep

15. Henry bought 4 dozen eggs. How many eggs did he buy?

A. 48 eggs   **B.** 60 eggs   **C.** 72 eggs   **D.** 84 eggs

16. Writing in Math Explain how you can find the quotient of $400 \div 10$.

_____

_____

_____

Translating Words to Expressions

Write a numerical expression for each word phrase.

1. 42 minus 10 baseballs _____

2. four times as many crayons as 4 colored pencils _____

3. $9 less than $25 _____

4. 15 toys given out equally to 5 students _____

5. 12 times as long as 2 in. _____

6. 4 people sharing 8 rolls equally _____

There are 12 cups in one package. Write a numerical expression
for how many there will be when there are

7. 2 fewer cups. _____

8. 8 more cups. _____

9. 6 times as many cups. _____

10. half the number of cups. _____

Choose the numerical expression that matches the situation.

11. Karl eats all 5 of his carrots.

    A. 5 + 5

    B. 5 − 5

12. Both cats receive 10 oz of food.

    A. 10 ÷ 2

    B. 10 × 2

13. Writing in Math Write two situations that would use the
numerical expression 27 ÷ 9.

_____

_____

_____

Name _____

The Dividing Life

Solve. Write your answer in a complete sentence.

1. Bailey is collecting dimes. She has 4 quarters. If Bailey changes her quarters for dimes at the bank, how many dimes will she get?

_____

2. At the zoo, there are 8 elephants and 2 trainers. How many elephants does each trainer work with if they both work with the same number of elephants?

_____

3. There are 16 oz in a pound of butter. While making bread, Andre read that he needs half that amount for the recipe. How many ounces does Andre need?

_____

4. Thomas has 3 boxes for toys in his room. He has 33 toys. If he divides the toys equally, how many toys will Thomas put into each box?

_____

5. Makayla has 32 books. She let each of her 4 friends borrow the same number of books. They borrowed all of Makayla's books. How many books did each friend borrow?

_____

6. Ms. Lucas has 19 paintbrushes for art class and 4 tables. If she puts an equal number of brushes on each table, how many brushes will be on each table? How many brushes will be left over?

_____

Solid Figures

Name the solid figure or figures each object looks like.

1.  _____

2. 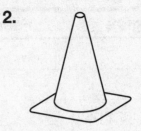 _____

3. 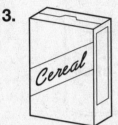 _____

4.  _____

5. What solid figures would you get if you cut a cube as shown?

_____

Test Prep

6. Which has the most flat surfaces?

A. Pyramid   **B.** Cylinder   **C.** Cone   **D.** Rectangular prism

7. Writing in Math Explain how a pyramid and a cone are alike and different.

_____

_____

_____

_____

Name_____

Relating Solids and Shapes

Complete the table.

Solid Figure	Faces	Edges	Corners
1. Cube			
2. Pyramid			
3. Rectangular prism			

4. How many flat surfaces does this coffee can have?

_____

Jane is making a building for her math project. How many corners does each combination of figures have?

5. 2 rectangular prisms

_____

6. 2 pyramids

_____

7. 2 cubes and 1 cylinder

_____

Test Prep

8. Which figure is NOT part of this object?

A. Sphere   **B.** Cylinder

C. Cone   **D.** Cube

9. **Writing in Math** How could you describe a cylinder to someone who has never seen one?

_____

_____

_____

_____

Name _____

Act It Out

Solve each problem by acting it out. Write the answer in
a complete sentence.

Kate built the 3 houses below with her building blocks.
How many blocks did she use for each house?

1. 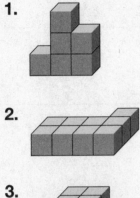 _____

2. 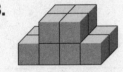 _____

3. _____

Jamie and Peter are playing a rhythm game. Every time Jamie
claps his hands, Peter stomps his feet twice.

4. After Jamie has clapped his hands 8 times, how many
times has Peter stomped his feet?

_____

5. If Peter stomps his feet 12 times, how many times does
Jamie clap his hands?

_____

6. If pencils were sold 4 to a pack, how many would be in 6 packs?

_____

7. Decision Making You are going to buy twice as many
pencils as someone who has 8 pencils. How many packs
of pencils will you buy?

_____

Name _____

Lines and Line Segments

Write the name for each.

1.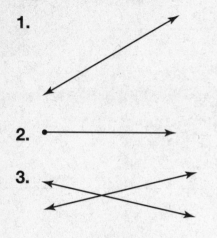

_____

2. _____

3. _____

4. Draw a set of parallel lines.

Use the map. Tell if the trails are parallel or intersecting.

5. Treetop and Sand Dune

_____

6. Sand Dune and Wildflower

_____

Treetop Trail

Nature
Center

Wildflower Trail

Sand Dune Trail

Test Prep

7. How many times does a pair of intersecting lines cross?

   A. Never   **B.** 1 time   **C.** 2 times   **D.** 3 times

8. **Writing in Math** Explain how you can tell the difference between a ray and a line.

_____

_____

Angles

Tell whether each angle is right, acute, or obtuse.

1. _____

2. _____

3. _____

4. _____

5. Draw a right angle. Then draw an acute angle and an obtuse angle.

Test Prep

6. At which time do the hands of a clock form an acute angle?

A. 2:00 P.M.   **B.** 4:00 P.M.   **C.** 6:00 P.M.   **D.** 8:00 P.M.

7. Writing in Math Describe an object that has a right angle.

_____

_____

_____

_____

Polygons

Is each figure below a polygon? If it is a polygon, give its name.
If not, explain why.

1.

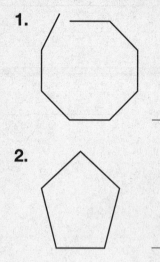

_____

2.

_____

Which polygon has

3. 6 sides? _____

4. 8 sides? _____

5. Reasoning Explain how you know the next polygon in the pattern.

_____

_____

Test Prep

6. Which is NOT a polygon?

A. Triangle   **B.** Pentagon   **C.** Circle   **D.** Hexagon

7. Writing in Math Explain why the shape of a football is not a polygon.

_____

_____

Triangles

Tell if each triangle is equilateral, isosceles, or scalene.

1.

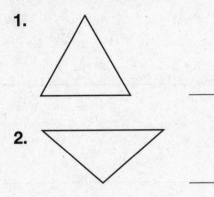 _____

2.

_____

Tell if each triangle is right, acute, or obtuse.

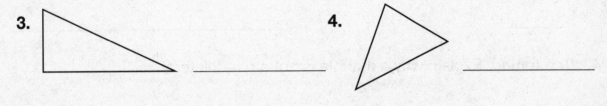

3. _____   **4.** _____

5. Draw an equilateral triangle.

Test Prep

6. Which best describes the triangle shown?

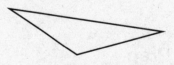

   A. Acute triangle, equilateral triangle

   B. Obtuse triangle, equilateral triangle

   C. Right triangle, scalene triangle

   D. Obtuse triangle, scalene triangle

7. Writing in Math Is it possible for an isosceles triangle to be an acute triangle? Explain.

_____

_____

Quadrilaterals

Write the name of each quadrilateral.

1.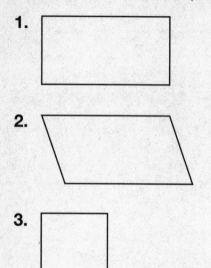

_____

2.

_____

3.

_____

4. **Reasoning** Explain why a triangle is not a quadrilateral.

_____

_____

5. Draw a quadrilateral with four equal sides, but no right angles. What is its name?

_____

Test Prep

6. Which of the following correctly names the figure?

   A. Rhombus   **B.** Trapezoid

   C. Parallelogram   **D.** Rectangle

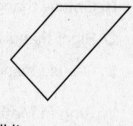

7. **Writing in Math** If you turn a rhombus upside down, will it still be a rhombus? Explain.

_____

_____

Congruent Figures and Motion

Are the figures congruent? Write *yes* or *no*.

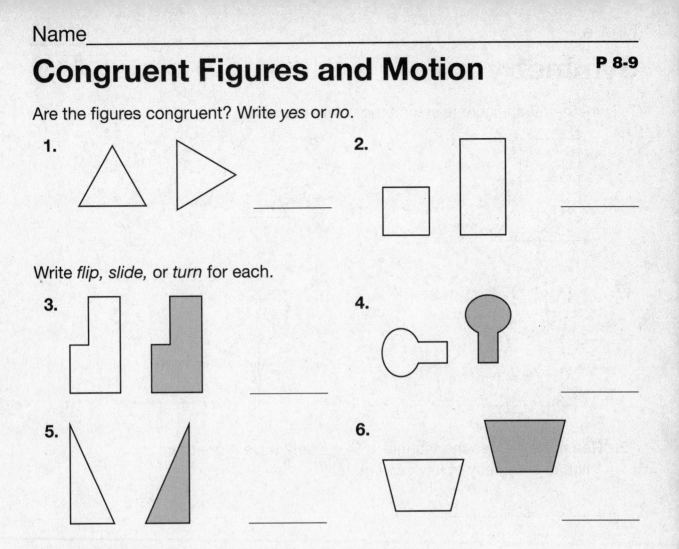

1.   _____

2.   _____

Write *flip, slide,* or *turn* for each.

3.   _____

4.   _____

5.   _____

6.   _____

7. **Reasoning** Are all squares congruent? Explain.

_____

_____

Test Prep

8. Which of the following are
   congruent figures?

   A. A and E   **B.** B and D

   C. C and F   **D.** A and F

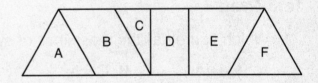

9. **Writing in Math** Could a triangle and a square ever be congruent?
   Explain.

_____

Symmetry

Tell whether each figure is symmetric. Write *yes* or *no*.

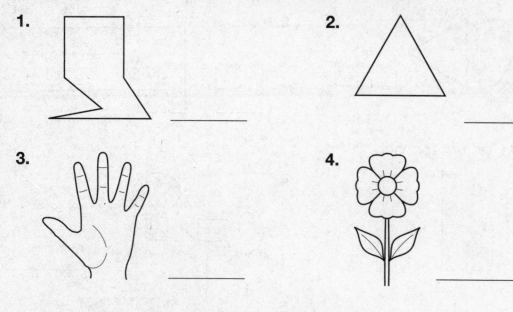

1. _____

2. _____

3. _____

4. _____

5. **Reasoning** Does the triangle in Exercise 2 have more than
   1 line of symmetry? How can you tell?

   _____

   _____

6. Tell how many lines of symmetry the figure
   at the right has. Draw the lines of symmetry.

   _____

Test Prep

7. Which figure has the most lines of symmetry?

   A. Square   **B.** Circle   **C.** Triangle   **D.** Hexagon

8. **Writing in Math** Can a chair be symmetric? Explain.

   _____

   _____

Perimeter

Find the perimeter of each polygon.

1. 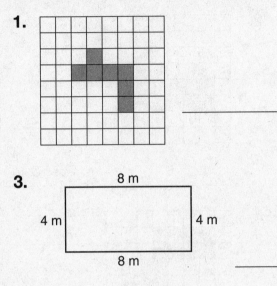 _____

2. 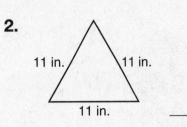 _____

3.

8 m

4 m   4 m

8 m   _____

4.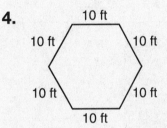

10 ft

10 ft   10 ft

10 ft   10 ft

10 ft   _____

Draw a figure with the given perimeter.

5. 10 units

6. 22 units

Test Prep

7. Which is the best estimate for the perimeter of your math book?

A. 5 in.   **B.** 10 ft   **C.** 25 in.   **D.** 25 ft

8. **Writing in Math** Explain how you could use grid paper to draw a rectangle with a perimeter of 18 units.

_____

_____

_____

Name

Area

Find the area of each figure. Write your answer in square units.

1.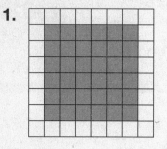

_____

2.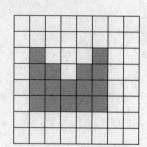

_____

3.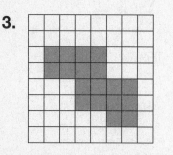

_____

4.

_____

5. **Reasoning** Use the grid. Draw two different figures that each have a perimeter of 14. Find each area.

Test Prep

6. Which is the area of this figure?

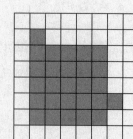

   A. 27 square units   **B.** 26 square units

   C. 25 square units   **D.** 24 square units

7. **Writing in Math** Explain why it would be important to know the area of a room that new furniture will be going into.

_____

Name_____

Volume

Find the volume of each figure. Write your answer in cubic units.

1.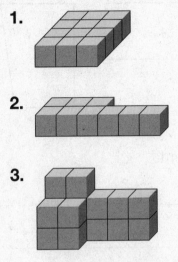

_____

2.

_____

3.

_____

4.

_____

5. Estimate the volume of the cube in cubic units.

_____

6. Kevin made a rectangular prism with 8 cubes in each layer. The prism had 4 layers. What is the volume of the rectangular prisms?

_____

Test Prep

7. Which is the volume of this figure?

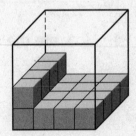

   A. 15 cubic units **B.** 20 cubic units

   C. 30 cubic units **D.** 35 cubic units

8. Writing in Math Explain how you found the volume of the figure in Exercise 7.

_____

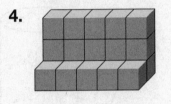

Name_____

Writing to Describe

1. Write a statement to describe how
A and B are alike.

_____

_____

2. Write a statement describing how A and B are different.

_____

_____

3. How are the cone and the cylinder alike?

_____

_____

4. How are the cone and the cylinder different?

_____

_____

5. Tina turned a parallelogram as shown. How are
the two parallelograms alike? How are they different?

_____

_____

_____

6. Reasoning I am a solid figure. My faces are quadrilaterals.
Two faces are squares. What am I?

_____

PROBLEM-SOLVING APPLICATIONS   **P 8-15**
Polygons and Volume

Use the figure for Exercises 1–4.

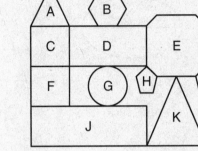

1. How many polygons are there in the figure?
   Do not count ones that overlap.

   _____

2. What kind of polygon is Figure B?

   _____

3. Are Figures H and I congruent? Explain.

   _____

   _____

   _____

4. Jeff says that Figures C and F have the same area. Do you
   agree? Explain.

   _____

   _____

   _____

5. Karen made a robot model out of cubes.
   What is the volume of the robot?

   _____

Equal Parts of a Whole

Tell if each shows equal parts or unequal parts.

1.

2.

3.

4.

_____   _____   _____   _____

Name the equal parts of the whole.

5.

6.

7.

_____   _____   _____

8.

9.

10.

_____   _____   _____

11. Amanda's grandmother made a quilt for Amanda's bed.
The quilt was made of 9 squares. Each square was
2 ft wide. How wide was Amanda's quilt?   _____

Test Prep

12. Which is the name of 12 equal parts of a whole?

A. Sixths   **B.** Twelfths   **C.** Halves   **D.** Tenths

13. **Writing in Math** Amanda says her quilt has 9 equal parts. Jeremy
says it has 3 equal parts. Can they both be correct? Explain.

_____

Naming Fractional Parts

Write the fraction of each figure that is shaded.

1. 　　　　　2. 　　　　　3. 　　　　　4.

_____　　_____　　_____　　_____

Draw a picture to show each fraction.

5. $\frac{1}{3}$ 　　　　　**6.** three eighths 　　　　　**7.** one fourth

Valerie and Austin went bowling. They tried to knock down 10 pins with a bowling ball. Valerie knocked down 7 pins on her first turn. Austin knocked down 4 pins on his turn. Use this information for Exercises 8–11.

8. What fraction of the pins did Valerie knock down? _____

9. Reasoning What fraction of Austin's pins were still standing after his turn? _____

Test Prep

10. Which fraction shows the number of pins still standing after Valerie's turn?

A. $\frac{9}{10}$ 　　　　　**B.** $\frac{7}{10}$ 　　　　　**C.** $\frac{5}{10}$ 　　　　　**D.** $\frac{3}{10}$

11. Writing in Math Clare decided to bowl after Austin. She knocked down 5 pins. Explain how you can find what fraction of the pins are still standing.

_____

_____

Equivalent Fractions

Complete each number sentence.

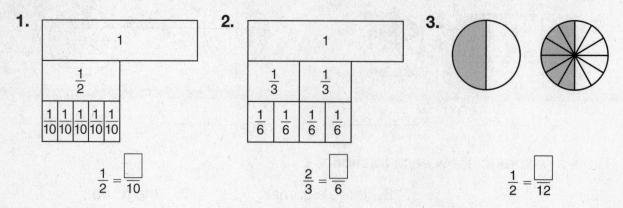

1. $\frac{1}{2} = \frac{\boxed{}}{10}$

2. $\frac{2}{3} = \frac{\boxed{}}{6}$

3. $\frac{1}{2} = \frac{\boxed{}}{12}$

4. **Reasoning** Samuel has read $\frac{5}{6}$ of his assignment. Judy has read $\frac{10}{12}$ of her assignment. Who has read more? Explain.

_____

_____

5. One half of the square is shaded. Draw three more ways to show $\frac{1}{2}$.

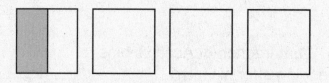

Test Prep

6. Which completes the pattern? $\frac{2}{3} = \frac{4}{6} = \frac{6}{9} = \frac{8}{12} = \frac{10}{\blacksquare}$

   A. 4   **B.** 8   **C.** 12   **D.** 15

7. **Writing in Math** Amy finished $\frac{6}{12}$ of the problems on her timed test. Jackson finished $\frac{4}{6}$ of the problems on the timed test. Did they finish the same fraction of the problems? Explain.

_____

_____

Comparing and Ordering Fractions

Compare. Write >, <, or =.

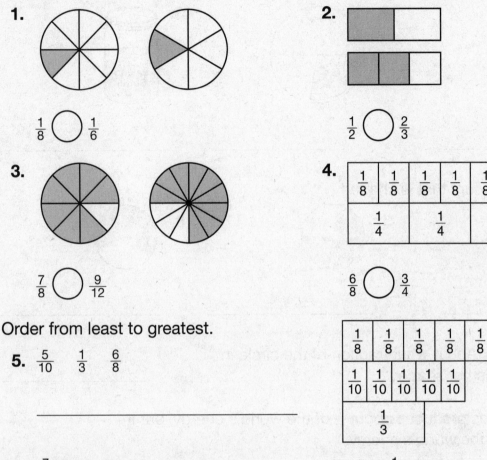

1. $\frac{1}{8} \bigcirc \frac{1}{6}$

2. $\frac{1}{2} \bigcirc \frac{2}{3}$

3. $\frac{7}{8} \bigcirc \frac{9}{12}$

4. $\frac{6}{8} \bigcirc \frac{3}{4}$

Order from least to greatest.

5. $\frac{5}{10}$ $\frac{1}{3}$ $\frac{6}{8}$

_____

6. $\frac{7}{10}$ of your body is made of water. Is more than $\frac{1}{2}$ of your body water? Explain.

_____

_____

Test Prep

7. Which fraction is equal to $\frac{1}{5}$?

   A. $\frac{2}{10}$ B. $\frac{3}{10}$ C. $\frac{1}{15}$ D. $\frac{2}{15}$

8. **Writing in Math** Explain why $\frac{1}{8}$ is greater than $\frac{1}{10}$, but less than $\frac{1}{3}$.

_____

_____

Estimating Fractional Amounts

Estimate the amount that is left.

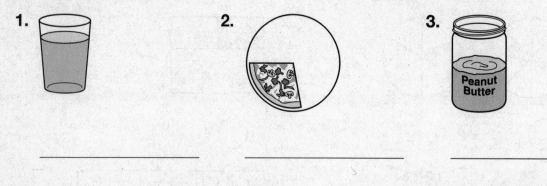

1. _____   2. _____   3. _____

Estimate the amount that is shaded.

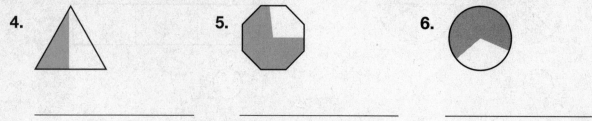

4. _____   5. _____   6. _____

7. **Reasoning** About what fraction of the circle in
   Exercise 6 is not shaded?   _____

The United States produces about $\frac{1}{5}$ of the world's energy, but it
uses about $\frac{1}{4}$ of the world's energy.

8. Draw a rectangle and shade it to show the
   fraction of the world's energy the United
   States produces.

Test Prep

9. About how much is shaded?

   A. $\frac{1}{5}$ B. $\frac{1}{8}$

   C. $\frac{1}{3}$ D. $\frac{2}{3}$

   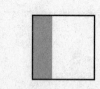

10. **Writing in Math** Draw a rectangle and shade
    about three-fourths of it. Write a fraction for the
    shaded and the unshaded parts.   _____

Name _____

Fractions on the Number Line

P 9-6

Write the missing fractions for each number line.

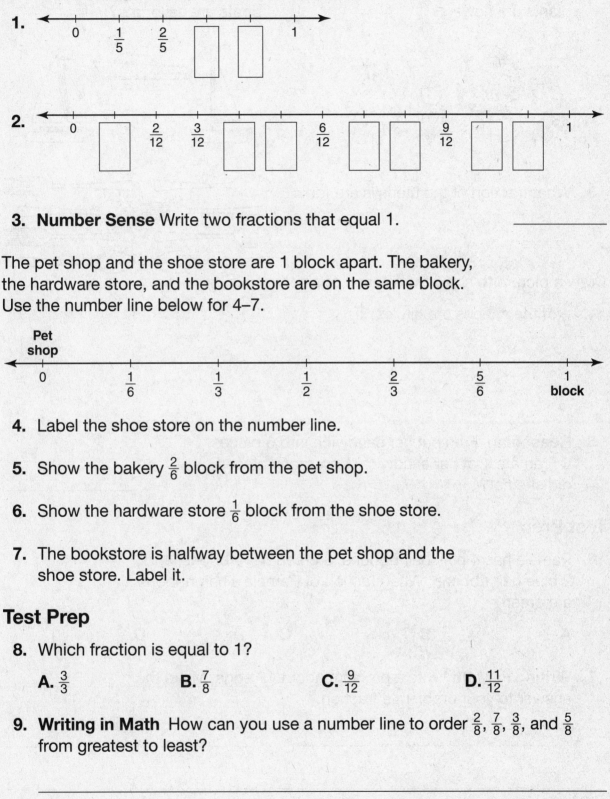

1.

2.

3. **Number Sense** Write two fractions that equal 1. _____

The pet shop and the shoe store are 1 block apart. The bakery,
the hardware store, and the bookstore are on the same block.
Use the number line below for 4–7.

4. Label the shoe store on the number line.

5. Show the bakery $\frac{2}{6}$ block from the pet shop.

6. Show the hardware store $\frac{1}{6}$ block from the shoe store.

7. The bookstore is halfway between the pet shop and the
shoe store. Label it.

Test Prep

8. Which fraction is equal to 1?

   A. $\frac{3}{3}$
   B. $\frac{7}{8}$
   C. $\frac{9}{12}$
   D. $\frac{11}{12}$

9. **Writing in Math** How can you use a number line to order $\frac{2}{8}$, $\frac{7}{8}$, $\frac{3}{8}$, and $\frac{5}{8}$
   from greatest to least?

   _____

   _____

© Pearson Education, Inc. 3

Fractions and Sets

1. What fraction of the plants are flowers? _____

2. What fraction of the boats are sailboats? _____

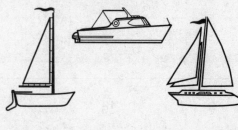

3. What fraction of the utensils are forks?

_____

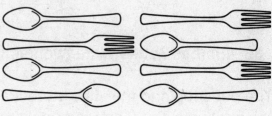

Draw a picture to show the fraction of a set.

4. $\frac{3}{5}$ of the shapes are circles.

5. Reasoning Fran cut her sandwich into 6 pieces. If Fran ate $\frac{1}{3}$ of her sandwich, how many pieces did she eat? _____

Test Prep

6. Pamela has 4 pink hair ribbons, 3 green hair ribbons, and 2 blue hair ribbons. What fraction of Pamela's hair ribbons are green?

A. $\frac{4}{5}$ **B.** $\frac{3}{4}$ **C.** $\frac{3}{6}$ **D.** $\frac{3}{9}$

7. Writing in Math Write a problem about 12 eggs. Make the answer to your problem a fraction.

_____

_____

_____

Finding Fractional Parts of a Set

1. Find $\frac{1}{3}$ of 9 books.

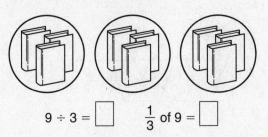

$9 \div 3 = \boxed{}$ $\frac{1}{3}$ of $9 = \boxed{}$

2. Find $\frac{1}{6}$ of 12 pencils.

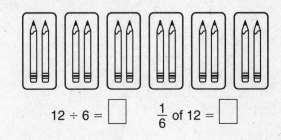

$12 \div 6 = \boxed{}$ $\frac{1}{6}$ of $12 = \boxed{}$

3. Find $\frac{1}{5}$ of 10. _____

4. Find $\frac{1}{2}$ of 18. _____

5. Find $\frac{1}{3}$ of 21. _____

6. Find $\frac{1}{4}$ of 20. _____

7. Number Sense To find $\frac{1}{3}$ of 24, what two numbers should you divide?

_____

8. April spent $\frac{1}{2}$ of a dollar in quarters. How many quarters did she spend?   _____

9. Justin found $\frac{1}{5}$ of a dollar in dimes. How many dimes did he find?   _____

10. Alex had 12 eggs. He used $\frac{1}{4}$ of them in an omelet. How many eggs did he use?   _____

11. Hannah used $\frac{1}{3}$ yd of ribbon to wrap a package. How many inches did she use? (Hint: There are 36 in. in 1 yd.)   _____

Test Prep

12. Which is $\frac{1}{8}$ of 64?

A. 8   **B.** 10   **C.** 12   **D.** 14

13. Writing in Math Draw a picture to show $\frac{1}{5}$ of 25.

Adding and Subtracting Fractions

Add or subtract. You may use fraction strips or draw a picture to help.

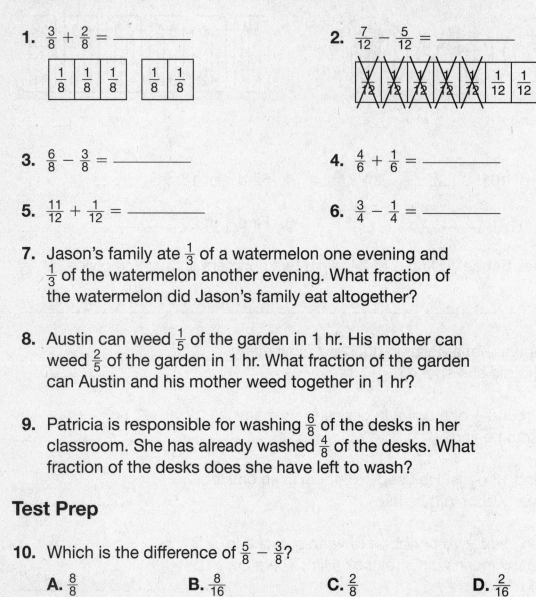

1. $\frac{3}{8} + \frac{2}{8} =$ _____

2. $\frac{7}{12} - \frac{5}{12} =$ _____

3. $\frac{6}{8} - \frac{3}{8} =$ _____

4. $\frac{4}{6} + \frac{1}{6} =$ _____

5. $\frac{11}{12} + \frac{1}{12} =$ _____

6. $\frac{3}{4} - \frac{1}{4} =$ _____

7. Jason's family ate $\frac{1}{3}$ of a watermelon one evening and $\frac{1}{3}$ of the watermelon another evening. What fraction of the watermelon did Jason's family eat altogether? _____

8. Austin can weed $\frac{1}{5}$ of the garden in 1 hr. His mother can weed $\frac{2}{5}$ of the garden in 1 hr. What fraction of the garden can Austin and his mother weed together in 1 hr? _____

9. Patricia is responsible for washing $\frac{6}{8}$ of the desks in her classroom. She has already washed $\frac{4}{8}$ of the desks. What fraction of the desks does she have left to wash? _____

Test Prep

10. Which is the difference of $\frac{5}{8} - \frac{3}{8}$?

A. $\frac{8}{8}$ **B.** $\frac{8}{16}$ **C.** $\frac{2}{8}$ **D.** $\frac{2}{16}$

11. **Writing in Math** Write an addition problem with $\frac{3}{5}$ as the sum.

_____

_____

_____

Mixed Numbers

Write a mixed number for each picture.

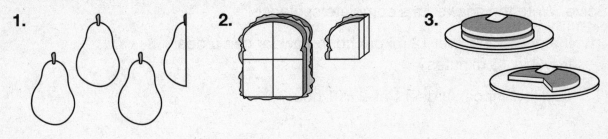

1.   2.   3.

_____   _____   _____

Draw a picture to show each number.

4. $2\frac{3}{4}$ **5.** $1\frac{2}{3}$

6. Number Sense Which is less, $3\frac{2}{3}$ or $3\frac{3}{4}$?   _____

7. Esther spent 2 hr swimming on Saturday afternoon.
She also spent $\frac{1}{2}$ hr writing letters. Write a mixed
number to show the total time Esther spent
swimming and writing letters.   _____

8. The black rhinoceros lives an average of 15 years.
How many decades does the rhinoceros live?
Write your answer as a mixed number. (Hint:
There are 10 years in a decade.)   _____

Test Prep

9. Which mixed number is greatest?

A. $1\frac{1}{2}$ **B.** $1\frac{1}{3}$ **C.** $1\frac{1}{4}$ **D.** $1\frac{2}{3}$

10. Writing in Math Tom said that 15 months is more than $1\frac{1}{2}$
years. Is he right? Explain.

_____

PROBLEM-SOLVING STRATEGY

Solve a Simpler Problem

Solve. Write the answer in a complete sentence.

1. If a deer can travel 12 mi per hour, how far can a deer travel in 15 minutes?

 a. How far can a deer travel in 1 hour?

 _____

 b. How many 15 min periods are in 1 hour?

 _____

 c. How can you find the distance a deer can travel in 15 minutes? Solve the problem.

 _____

2. How many diamonds are in the figure?

 _____

 _____

 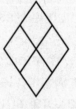

3. Hector's family began their vacation on July 3. First, they drove for 2 days. Then they stayed with relatives for 3 days. After visiting relatives, they drove a whole day to get to the ocean. They vacationed at the ocean for 5 days. It took them 3 days to drive back home. How many weeks was Hector's family gone?

 _____

4. Maria bought 13 comic books at a garage sale. She kept 4 comic books and divided the rest equally between some friends. Each friend got 3 comic books. With how many friends did Maria share the comic books?

 _____

Length

Estimate each length. Then measure to the nearest inch.

1.

_____

2.    **3.**

_____   _____

4. Measure the perimeter of the rectangle to the nearest inch.

_____

Test Prep

5. Measure the line segment to the nearest inch.

●————————————————●

A. 2 in.   **B.** 3 in.   **C.** 4 in.   **D.** 5 in.

6. Writing in Math Explain how to use a ruler to measure to the nearest inch.

_____

_____

_____

_____

Measuring to the Nearest $\frac{1}{2}$ and $\frac{1}{4}$ Inch

Measure the length of each object to the nearest $\frac{1}{2}$ and $\frac{1}{4}$ inch.

1.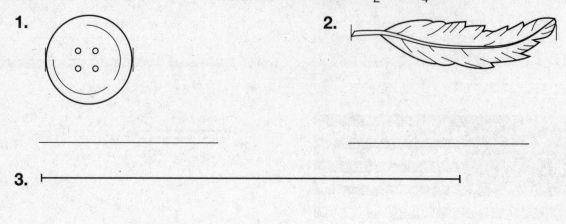

2.

_____   _____

3. |————————————————————————————|

_____

4. Draw a line segment that is $3\frac{3}{4}$ in. long.

5. **Estimation** Estimate the length of the pencil you are using to the nearest $\frac{1}{4}$ inch. Then measure to check. Record your estimate and measurement.

_____

Test Prep

6. Which can NOT be a length to the nearest $\frac{1}{4}$ inch?

   A. $\frac{1}{4}$ in.   **B.** $\frac{1}{2}$ in.   **C.** $\frac{3}{8}$ in.   **D.** 1 in.

7. **Writing in Math** Eric and Madison both measured the same trading card. Eric says the card is 3 in. long. Madison says it is $2\frac{3}{4}$ in. long. Their teacher says they are both correct. How is this possible?

_____

_____

_____

_____

Length in Feet and Inches

Write each measurement in inches. You may make a table to help.

1. 3 ft, 3 in. _____   **2.** 1 ft, 9 in. _____   **3.** 2 ft, 7 in. _____

4. 5 ft, 6 in. _____   **5.** 4 ft, 8 in. _____   **6.** 1 ft, 11 in. _____

7. Finish the table to find how many inches are in 7 ft, 8 in.
Write the answer in a complete sentence.

Feet	1	2	3	4	5	6	7
Inches							

_____

African elephant	13 ft tall
Whale shark	41 ft 6 in. long
Stick insect	1 ft 3 in. long
Giraffe	19 ft tall

8. How many inches long is the stick insect? _____

9. How many inches taller is a giraffe than an African elephant? _____

10. List the animals in order from largest to smallest.

_____

_____

Test Prep

11. Which measurement is equal to 3 ft, 7 in.?

A. 37 in.   **B.** 43 in.   **C.** 44 in.   **D.** 73 in.

12. **Writing in Math** Name something you would not measure
in feet and inches. Tell why.

_____

_____

Feet, Yards, and Miles

Change the units. You may make a table to help.

1. How many feet are in 7 yd?

_____

2. How many inches are in 2 yd?

_____

3. How many feet are in 5 yd?

_____

4. How many inches are in 3 yd?

_____

Compare. Write $<$, $>$, or $=$.

5. 90 in. $\bigcirc$ 3 yd

6. 1,800 yd $\bigcirc$ 1 mi

Circle the better estimate.

7. The depth of a swimming pool

10 ft or 10 mi

8. The length of your desk

2 ft or 2 yd

9. A baseball diamond has 90 ft between each base.
A softball diamond has 60 ft between each base.
How many yards longer is the space between
bases on a baseball diamond than a softball
diamond?   _____

Test Prep

10. Which unit would be best to measure the distance around
the equator?

A. Inches   **B.** Feet   **C.** Yards   **D.** Miles

11. **Writing in Math** Explain how to use multiplication to
convert yards to feet.

_____

_____

_____

PROBLEM-SOLVING SKILL

Extra or Missing Information

Decide if each problem has extra information or missing information. Solve if you have enough information.

1. Mrs. James wants to purchase new carpet for her bedroom. The carpet costs $13 per foot. Her bedroom is 5 ft shorter than the living room. How much carpet will she need?

_____

2. For each time Kendra walks Mr. Karl's dog, he gives her $3. Kendra walks the dog for 30 min each time. If she walks the dog on Monday, Tuesday, and Thursday, how much money does Kendra make each week for walking Mr. Karl's dog?

_____

_____

3. Dylan trades baseball cards with his friends. He received most of his baseball cards as a gift from his grandmother. If Dylan trades 58 baseball cards away and gets 62 back, how many more cards does he have now?

_____

_____

4. **Writing in Math** Write a story problem that does not have enough information. Use the grocery prices in your problem.

Groceries	
Bread	$2.29
Milk	$3.09
Cheese	$1.50
Orange juice	$3.25
Cereal	$4.79

_____

_____

_____

PROBLEM-SOLVING APPLICATION

Food Servings

The table shows an example of one serving of each of the food
groups in the food pyramid.

Group	Example of 1 Serving
Milk, yogurt, and cheese	$1\frac{1}{2}$ oz of cheese
Meat, beans, eggs, and nuts	$\frac{2}{3}$ c of nuts
Vegetables	$\frac{3}{4}$ c vegetable juice
Fruit	1 medium apple
Bread, cereal, and pasta	1 slice of bread

Solve. Write your answer in a complete sentence.

1. Patsy and Kyle each drank 1 serving of carrot juice. How
   many cups of carrot juice did they drink altogether?

   _____

   _____

2. Alex has $\frac{4}{5}$ c of walnuts. Does he have enough for
   1 serving? Explain.

   _____

   _____

3. Luke has $1\frac{3}{6}$ oz of cheese. He says that is enough for one
   serving. Do you agree? Explain.

   _____

   _____

4. A loaf of bread will provide 1 serving each for Julia and her
   brother for 5 days. How many slices of bread are in the loaf?

   _____

Name_____

Tenths

Write a fraction and a decimal for each shaded part.

1.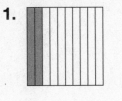

_____

2.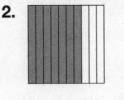

_____

3.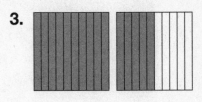

_____

Write each as a decimal.

4. $\frac{4}{10}$ _____

5. $7\frac{9}{10}$ _____

6. four and six tenths _____

7. eight tenths _____

8. Number Sense How many tenths are in 3.2? _____

9. It takes $8\frac{5}{10}$ min for light to get from the Sun to Earth. Write a decimal to show how long it takes.

_____

10. Sylvia has 10 beads with different shapes: 3 red beads are heart shaped, 2 blue beads are star shaped, and 5 white beads are cylinder shaped. Write a decimal for the number of red heart-shaped beads.

_____

Test Prep

11. How many tenths are in 0.2?

A. 22   **B.** 20   **C.** 12   **D.** 2

12. Writing in Math Explain how to find the mixed number and decimal for nine and one tenth.

_____

_____

_____

Hundredths

Write a fraction or mixed number and a decimal for each shaded part.

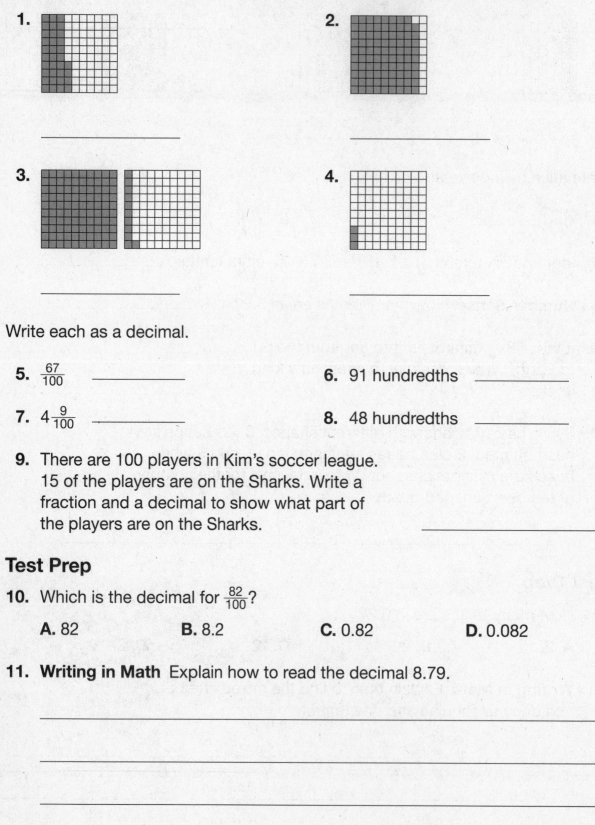

1.

_____

2.

_____

3.

_____

4.

_____

Write each as a decimal.

5. $\frac{67}{100}$ _____

6. 91 hundredths _____

7. $4\frac{9}{100}$ _____

8. 48 hundredths _____

9. There are 100 players in Kim's soccer league. 15 of the players are on the Sharks. Write a fraction and a decimal to show what part of the players are on the Sharks. _____

Test Prep

10. Which is the decimal for $\frac{82}{100}$?

    A. 82   **B.** 8.2   **C.** 0.82   **D.** 0.082

11. **Writing in Math** Explain how to read the decimal 8.79.

_____

_____

_____

Comparing and Ordering Decimals   P 10-3

Compare. Use <, >, or =.

1. 0.6 ◯ 0.60   **2.** 0.78 ◯ 0.68

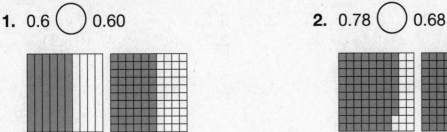

Use the number line to order the decimals from least to greatest.

0   0.05   0.1   0.15   0.2   0.25   0.3   0.35   0.4   0.45   0.5

3. 0.15   0.5   0.25   _____

4. 0.47   0.35   0.4   _____

Order the decimals from least to greatest.

5. 0.34   0.42   0.36   _____

6. 0.07   0.7   0.71   _____

Test Prep

7. On a number line, which of the following would come
between 0.12 and 0.2?

A. 0.09   **B.** 0.18   **C.** 0.22   **D.** 0.91

8. Writing in Math Explain how to compare 0.34 and 0.27.

_____

_____

_____

_____

_____

Adding and Subtracting Decimals

Add.

1.	0.9	2.	3.47	3.	3.1	4.	4.72
	+ 0.4		+ 1.14		+ 2.7		+ 5.81

Subtract.

5.	5.2	6.	9.51	7.	3.8	8.	8.78
	− 2.2		− 3.9		− 2.9		− 5.30

9. It is 3.41 mi from Kyle's house to the library. Michelle's house is 2.78 mi from the library. How much farther from the library is Kyle's house than Michelle's house?

_____

10. Sam bought a book at the bookstore for $6.97. Jasmine bought the same book for $3.74 on the Internet. How much more did Sam pay for the book than Jasmine?

_____

Test Prep

11. Which is the sum of 52.62 + 6.71?

A. 45.91　　　　**B.** 53.29　　　　**C.** 59.33　　　　**D.** 119.72

12. **Writing in Math** Without subtracting, tell which is greater, 2.3 − 1.7 or 1. Explain.

_____

_____

_____

Make an Organized List

Solve. Write the answer in a complete sentence.

1. How many ways can you arrange the letters A, B, C,
   and D? Continue the list to find all the ways.

   A B C D   B A C D
   A B D C   B A D C
   A C B D
   A C D B
   A D B C
   A D C B

   _____

   _____

2. Three marbles are in a jar: 1 red marble, 1 blue marble, and
   1 green marble. In how many different orders can you take
   the marbles out of the jar?

   _____

   _____

3. Beth's mother told her that she can choose 4 books from
   the book fair. There are 6 books that Beth would like to
   have. How many different combinations of 4 books could
   Beth choose from those 6?

   _____

   _____

4. Jim and Sarah are running for class president. Cayla and
   Daniel are running for vice president. How many
   combinations of students can be elected as class president
   and vice president?

   _____

   _____

Centimeters and Decimeters

Estimate each length. Then measure to the nearest centimeter.

1.  _____

2.  _____

3. **Number Sense** Without using a ruler, draw a line that is
9 cm long. Check your estimate by measuring.

4. Estimate the perimeter of your desk in centimeters.
Measure the perimeter to the nearest centimeter to check
your estimate.

_____

Test Prep

5. Measure the stapler to the nearest centimeter.

   A. 2 cm   **B.** 3 cm

   C. 4 cm   **D.** 5 cm

6. **Writing in Math** Explain how you can find the number of
centimeters in 6 dm.

_____

_____

_____

_____

_____

Meters and Kilometers

Choose the best estimate for each.

1. a key _____ **A.** 3 km

2. height of a door _____ **B.** 3 m

3. distance to the store _____ **C.** 3 cm

Tell if you would use meters or kilometers for each.

4. diameter of Earth _____

5. length of a store aisle _____

6. distance of a bus route _____

7. The northern border of the United States is about
6,416 km. The Great Wall of China is 6,350 km long.
Which is longer, and by how many kilometers?

_____

_____

8. Complete. Use patterns to find the missing numbers.

m	1,000	3,000	5,000	7,000	9,000
km	1				

Test Prep

9. Which is the best estimate for the length of a person's nose?

A. 5 ft   **B.** 5 cm   **C.** 5 m   **D.** 5 km

10. **Writing in Math** Is the length of your pencil greater than or
less than 1 m? Explain.

_____

_____

PROBLEM-SOLVING SKILL   P 10-8
Writing to Explain

Write to explain.

1. Explain how a tenth is related to a hundredth.

   _____

   _____

   _____

2. Explain how you can use three shapes
   to make the figure shown.

   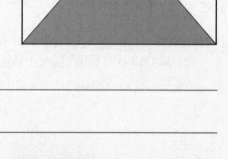

   _____

   _____

   _____

   _____

3. Explain how the 50 stars are arranged
   on the American flag.

   _____

   _____

   _____

   _____

4. Tell what part of the whole is shaded. Use tenths and
   hundredths in your explanation.

   _____

   _____

Name_____

Friends of the Forests

1. The boundary of the forest near Steven's house is 7 km
   long. How many meters long is the boundary?

   _____

2. The park in Cecilia's neighborhood has 3 different forest
   paths. Each path is about 400 m. Is the total of the 3 paths
   greater than or less than 1 km? Explain.

   _____

   _____

   _____

In the United States, forests and woodlands make up three
tenths of the land.

3. Write a decimal and fraction to show how much
   of the United States is forests and woodlands.　　_____

4. Henry is cutting a 120 cm long watermelon into equal
   slices for his family's picnic. Each slice is 5 cm. Complete
   the table.

Number of Slices	0	1	2	3	4
Watermelon Length	120	115			

   Explain how the length of the watermelon changes as the
   number of slices cut from the watermelon changes.

   _____

   _____

   _____

Mental Math: Multiplication Patterns

Use mental math to find each product.

1. $3 \times 10 =$ _____

2. $6 \times 100 =$ _____

3. $9 \times 1,000 =$ _____

4. $80 \times 3 =$ _____

5. $4 \times 700 =$ _____

6. $2,000 \times 5 =$ _____

7. $6 \times 400 =$ _____

8. $800 \times 8 =$ _____

9. $600 \times 9 =$ _____

Algebra Find the missing number in each number sentence.

10. $9 \times$ _____ $= 720$

11. _____ $\times 5,000 = 40,000$

12. The average workweek is 40 hr. How many hours are there in 4 workweeks? _____

13. There are 2,000 lb in 1 T. How many pounds are there in 16 T? _____

14. Lightning strikes the earth about 200 times each second. How many times does lightning strike the earth in 1 min? _____

Test Prep

15. How many hundreds are there in 2,000?

A. 2,000   **B.** 200   **C.** 20   **D.** 2

16. Writing in Math Explain how to use mental math to find 700×8.

_____

_____

_____

Estimating Products

Estimate each product.

1. 4 × 869 _____

2. 7 × 41 _____

3. 3 × 6,872 _____

4. 2 × 631 _____

5. 5 × 98 _____

6. 9 × 8,127 _____

7. 6 × 38 _____

8. 8 × 767 _____

9. Number Sense Cheryl has 3 weeks to finish a project. She knows that she can spend 2 hr a day on the project, and that it will take her about 40 hr. If Cheryl works on the project every day, does she have enough time to finish it?

_____

_____

_____

10. There are 365 days in 1 year. About how many days are there in 7 years?

_____

Test Prep

11. Which is the best estimate for 7 × 419?

A. 2,100 **B.** 2,800 **C.** 3,500 **D.** 4,000

12. Writing in Math There are 5,280 ft in 1 mi. Explain how you can tell if there are at least 25,000 ft in 5 mi.

_____

_____

_____

Mental Math: Division Patterns

Use patterns to find each quotient.

1. $18 \div 3 =$ _____

$180 \div 3 =$ _____

$1,800 \div 3 =$ _____

2. $36 \div 4 =$ _____

$360 \div 4 =$ _____

$3,600 \div 4 =$ _____

Use mental math to find each quotient.

3. $200 \div 5 =$ _____ **4.** $3,600 \div 6 =$ _____ **5.** $2,700 \div 3 =$ _____

6. $490 \div 7 =$ _____ **7.** $1,200 \div 2 =$ _____ **8.** $630 \div 9 =$ _____

Algebra Use mental math to find the missing numbers.

9. $810 \div$ _____ $= 90$

10. _____ $\div 2 = 800$

11. _____ $\div 7 = 500$

12. $4,200 \div$ _____ $= 600$

13. There are 5 reams of paper in a box. There are
2,500 pages total in the box. How many sheets
of paper are in 1 ream of paper?   _____

Test Prep

14. Use mental math to find the quotient of $480 \div 8$.

A. 6   **B.** 8   **C.** 60   **D.** 80

15. **Writing in Math** Explain how you can find the quotient
for $120,000 \div 3$ using mental math.

_____

_____

_____

_____

Estimating Quotients

Estimate each quotient.

1. 66 ÷ 8 _____

2. 31 ÷ 6 _____

3. 19 ÷ 2 _____

4. 23 ÷ 4 _____

5. 22 ÷ 6 _____

6. 43 ÷ 7 _____

7. 70 ÷ 8 _____

8. 19 ÷ 4 _____

9. A group of students is sharing 62 markers. If there are
7 students, about how many markers will each student have?

_____

10. James has 6 pencils. His father has 44 pencils. About how
many times more pencils does James's father have?

_____

11. Number Sense Without finding the exact answer, how do
you know that 41 ÷ 5 is greater than 40 ÷ 5?

_____

_____

Test Prep

12. Which is the best estimate for 37 ÷ 5?

A. 5 **B.** 6 **C.** 7 **D.** 8

13. Writing in Math Frances has 37 c of apples to make loaves
of apple bread. If each loaf uses 4 c of apples, explain how
Frances can find about how many loaves she can make.

_____

_____

_____

Multiplication and Arrays

Find each product. You may draw a picture to help.

1. $3 \times 17 =$ _____

2. $2 \times 22 =$ _____

3. $5 \times 34 =$ _____   **4.** $4 \times 13 =$ _____   **5.** $3 \times 57 =$ _____

6. Reasoning Draw an array to show the number
of eggs in 3 dozens.   _____

Each worker is paid $8 per hour of work.

Worker	Hours Worked
Bob	19
Josh	35
Marvin	13

7. How many dollars did Bob earn?

_____

8. How many dollars did Josh earn?   _____

9. How much more did Bob earn than Marvin?   _____

Test Prep

10. Which is the product of 52×6?

A. 42   **B.** 302   **C.** 312   **D.** 402

11. Writing in Math Explain how to use an array to find 3×19.

_____

Name _____

Breaking Numbers Apart to Multiply

Find each product.

1. 63
   × 4

2. 18
   × 7

3. $42
   × 9

4. 88
   × 2

5. 2 × 72 = _____

6. 3 × 49 = _____

7. 6 × 31 = _____

8. 3 × 82 = _____

9. Each wood panel is 6 ft wide. Exactly 19 panels are needed to cover the walls of a room. What is the perimeter of the room?

_____

10. A carpenter makes chairs with slats that run across the back of the chairs as shown. Each chair uses 7 slats. He needs to make 36 chairs. How many slats must he make?

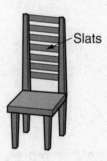

Slats

_____

Test Prep

11. Which is the same as 5 × 25?

A. 25 + 10   **B.** 105   **C.** 30   **D.** 100 + 25

12. Writing in Math Susie says, "I can find 12 × 8 by adding 80 and 16." Do you agree? Why or why not?

_____

_____

_____

_____

_____

Multiplying Two-Digit Numbers

Find each product. Decide if your answer is reasonable.

1. $\begin{array}{r} 12 \\ \times\ \ 9 \\ \hline \end{array}$	**2.** $\begin{array}{r} 19 \\ \times\ \ 4 \\ \hline \end{array}$	**3.** $\begin{array}{r} \$22 \\ \times\ \ 7 \\ \hline \end{array}$	**4.** $\begin{array}{r} 45 \\ \times\ \ 6 \\ \hline \end{array}$

5. $\begin{array}{r} 96 \\ \times\ \ 3 \\ \hline \end{array}$	**6.** $\begin{array}{r} 27 \\ \times\ \ 5 \\ \hline \end{array}$	**7.** $\begin{array}{r} 12 \\ \times\ \ 8 \\ \hline \end{array}$	**8.** $\begin{array}{r} \$55 \\ \times\ \ 4 \\ \hline \end{array}$

9. $\begin{array}{r} 9 \\ \times\ \$36 \\ \hline \end{array}$	**10.** $\begin{array}{r} 37 \\ \times\ \ 4 \\ \hline \end{array}$	**11.** $\begin{array}{r} 82 \\ \times\ \ 6 \\ \hline \end{array}$	**12.** $\begin{array}{r} \$71 \\ \times\ \ 7 \\ \hline \end{array}$

13. $14 \times 5 =$ _____

14. $6 \times 51 =$ _____

15. $63 \times 4 =$ _____

16. $\$47 \times 2 =$ _____

17. An area in Norway gets sunlight all day for 14 weeks straight during the summer. How many days of continuous sunlight is this? _____

18. The length of a parking lot is 92 yd. How many feet long is the parking lot? _____

Test Prep

19. Which is the product of $82 \times \$7$?

A. $434   **B.** $494   **C.** $564   **D.** $574

20. **Writing in Math** Explain how an array of 5×46 can help you find the product of 5×46.

_____

_____

_____

Multiplying Three-Digit Numbers

Find each answer. Estimate to check reasonableness.

1. 231
    × 2

2. 420
    × 3

3. 613
    × 5

4. 122
    × 8

5. 308
    × 7

6. 501
    × 8

7. 727
    × 4

8. 914
    × 9

9. 444 × 4 = _____

10. 121 × 6 = _____

11. There are 365 days in 1 year. How many days
    are there in 3 years?   _____

12. A board is 144 in. long. How many inches long
    are 8 boards?   _____

13. **Number Sense** Is 721 × 3 the same as 2,100 + 60 + 3? Explain.

    _____

    _____

Test Prep

14. Which is the product of 828 × 5?

    A. 4,040   **B.** 4,100   **C.** 4,140   **D.** 4,840

15. **Writing in Math** Larry multiplied 362 × 4.
    Explain Larry's error and give the correct answer.

    $$\begin{array}{r} {}^{2}\,362 \\ \times\ 4 \\ \hline 1{,}248 \end{array}$$

    _____

    _____

    _____

Multiplying Money

Find each product. Estimate to check reasonableness.

1. $1.32
    × 6

2. $4.67
    × 4

3. $6.04
    × 9

4. $4.21
    × 2

5. $7.49
    × 3

6. $5.08
    × 7

7. $8.29
    × 3

8. $5.65
    × 8

9. $6.78 × 1 = _____

10. $7.90 × 4 = _____

11. $3.22 × 5 = _____

12. How much is 4 gal of milk?

    _____

13. How much is 6 bagels?

    _____

14. How much is 7 gal of gas?

    _____

```
┌─────────────────────────────┐
│  Fast Gas                    │
│  Gas/gallon          $1.37   │
├─────────────────────────────┤
│  Come inside!                │
│  Milk gallon ..........  $2.49 │
│  Bread ................  $0.99 │
│  Bagels ...............  2/$1.89│
└─────────────────────────────┘
```

Test Prep

15. If wallpaper is $8.27 a roll, which is the cost of 8 rolls?

    A. $48.62   **B.** $62.76   **C.** $66.16   **D.** $78.22

16. **Writing in Math** Explain how to find the product of
     $7.50 × 8.

    _____

    _____

    _____

Choose a Computation Method

Find each product. Tell which computation method you used.

1. $9.07 × 4	2. 500 × 3	3. 3,678 × 9	4. 619 × 7

_____ _____ _____ _____

5. 7,234 × 7 = _____   6. 8,000 × 4 = _____

_____   _____

7. **Number Sense** Explain which computation method you would choose to multiply $4.32 × 6.

_____

_____

8. Celia sent 4 packages out through the mail. Three of them had postage of $6.32 and one was $7.51. How much was the postage altogether?   _____

Test Prep

9. Which is the product of 811 × 9?

A. 72,990   **B.** 7,299   **C.** 7,209   **D.** 7,200

10. **Writing in Math** Explain when it is best to use a calculator to solve a problem.

_____

_____

_____

_____

PROBLEM-SOLVING STRATEGY   **P 11-11**

Use Logical Reasoning

Solve. Write the answer in a complete sentence.

1. Complete the table. Then use the table to find what color uniform the Wolves wear.

_____

   • The Bears do not wear red or green.
   • The Cougars wear white.
   • There is no green on the Pumas' uniforms.

	Bears	Cougars	Pumas	Wolves
Blue				
Green				
Red				
White				

2. Sally has an appointment on Thursday. The first appointment of the day is at 9 A.M. and the final one is at 3 P.M. Sally's appointment is not the first of the day or the last. Her appointment is on the hour. The sum of the digits in the hour is 3. What time is Sally's appointment?

_____

3. I am an odd number with 3 digits. The sum of my digits is 5. My first and last digits are the same. What number am I?

_____

4. Ben's grandfather is 5 times as old as Ben. Ben's father is 22 years younger than his grandfather. If Ben is 12 years old, how old is Ben's father?

_____

Using Objects to Divide

Use place-value blocks or draw a picture to find each quotient.

1. $64 \div 4 =$ _____   **2.** $94 \div 2 =$ _____

3. $51 \div 3 =$ _____   **4.** $80 \div 5 =$ _____

5. $91 \div 7 =$ _____   **6.** $80 \div 8 =$ _____

7. $96 \div 8 =$ _____   **8.** $87 \div 3 =$ _____

9. $88 \div 4 =$ _____   **10.** $57 \div 3 =$ _____

11. Trisha collected 4 times as many bugs as
Shirley. If Trisha collected 60 bugs, how
many did Shirley collect?   _____

12. Candice bought a box of books for $78.
There are 6 books in a box. If they all cost the
same, how much did each book cost?   _____

Test Prep

13. Which is the quotient of $630 \div 9$?

A. 7   **B.** 8   **C.** 60   **D.** 70

14. **Writing in Math** Explain how you could use a picture to
help you solve $81 \div 3$.

_____

_____

_____

_____

_____

Breaking Numbers Apart to Divide   **P 11-13**

Use the break apart method to find each quotient. You may draw a picture to help.

1. $60 \div 3 =$ _____

2. $60 \div 4 =$ _____

3. $72 \div 3 =$ _____

4. $95 \div 5 =$ _____

5. $4\overline{)64}$ **6.** $2\overline{)64}$ **7.** $2\overline{)32}$ **8.** $3\overline{)48}$

9. Jennifer has 57 fish in one tank. She wants to move them to 3 smaller tanks. If she puts the same number of fish in each of the 3 smaller tanks, how many fish will be in each tank?   _____

10. There is enough room for 5 rows of chairs in a room. There are 75 people to be seated. How many chairs must be in each row?   _____

Test Prep

11. Which has the greatest quotient?

A. $75 \div 3$ **B.** $96 \div 4$ **C.** $82 \div 2$ **D.** $48 \div 3$

12. **Writing in Math** Explain how using the break apart method can help you solve $84 \div 4$.

_____

_____

_____

Dividing

Complete. Check your answer.

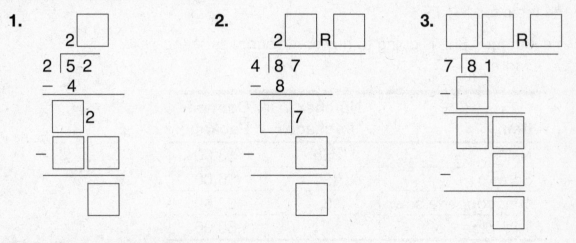

Divide. Check your answers.

4. 7)91   **5.** 4)35   **6.** 5)46   **7.** 2)71

8. A set of bleachers will seat 72 people. If each bench in the bleachers seats 6 people, how many benches are there?

_____

9. Lana has 80 beads. She is making bracelets that use 7 beads each. How many bracelets can she complete?

_____

Test Prep

10. How many 8s can you take out of 94?

A. 13   **B.** 12   **C.** 11   **D.** 10

11. Writing in Math Maureen divided 72 by 3. Is her work correct? If not, tell why and give the correct answer.

_____

_____

_____

$$\begin{array}{r} 114 \\ 3\overline{)72} \\ \underline{3} \\ 42 \\ \underline{42} \\ 0 \end{array}$$

PROBLEM-SOLVING SKILL

Interpreting Remainders

Use the table for 1–4.

Gail is a plumber. She is going to buy some supplies at the hardware store.

Item	Number in Package	Cost per Package
Nails	50	$3.00
Screws	25	$6.00
1 in. copper elbow	3	$2.50
1 in. pipe – 6 ft	1	$5.00

1. How many packages of copper elbows should Gail buy if she needs 41 elbows?

   _____

2. How many packages of nails can Gail buy with $74.00?

   _____

3. How many packages of screws can Gail buy with $52.00?

   _____

4. If Gail started with $76.00 and bought as many pipes as she could, how much money would she have left?

   _____

5. Skyler has 47 apples. There are 3 people in his family. If each person ate the same number of apples, how many have they each eaten? How many apples are left?

   _____

   _____

Sleep Time

Solve. Write the answer in a complete sentence.

Average Sleep per Day

Animal	Hours
Elephant	2
Gorilla	14
Human	8
Sloth	18

1. How many minutes does a human sleep per day?

_____

2. How many hours does an elephant sleep per year?

_____

3. How many hours does a sloth sleep per week?

_____

4. How many days will it take for a human to sleep 99 hr?

_____

_____

5. Midge is leaving for a trip in June. It is not on a weekday. The sum of the date's digits is 8. On what date is Midge leaving for her trip?

June						
S	M	T	W	T	F	S
		1	2	3	4	5
6	7	8	9	10	11	12
13	14	15	16	17	18	19
20	21	22	23	24	25	26
27	28	29	30			

_____

_____

Customary Units of Capacity

Estimate Choose the better estimate for each.

1.

1 c or 1 gal _____

2.

3 pt or 3 qt _____

Find the missing number.

3. 2 gal = _____ qt   **4.** 8 qt = _____ pt   **5.** 32 c = _____ gal

6. 12 pt = _____ qt   **7.** 5 gal = _____ pt   **8.** 2 qt = _____ c

9. Which is less, 7 c of water or 3 qt of water? _____

10. **Number Sense** How many cups are in 1 qt 1 pt? _____

11. A 10 gal fish tank with 12 fish in it needs $\frac{1}{2}$ of its water
replaced every 2 weeks. How many quarts of water need
to be replaced? _____

12. There is about 10 pt of blood in the human body. How
many quarts of blood are there? _____

Test Prep

13. How many gallons are there in 40 qt?

A. 160   **B.** 80   **C.** 20   **D.** 10

14. **Writing in Math** Explain how you found the answer for
Exercise 11.

_____

_____

Milliliters and Liters

Estimation Choose the better estimate for each.

1.

250 mL or 1 L _____

2.

4 L or 40 mL _____

3. Which is less, 3,500 mL of oil or 3 L of oil?   _____

Compare. Use >, <, or =.

4. 10 L $\bigcirc$ 10,000 mL

5. 8,000 mL $\bigcirc$ 7 L

6. A jug holds 6 L of water. If there are 4 people using the jug, how many milliliters of water can each have?

_____

7. From a 2 L container of juice, 750 mL is spilled. How much juice is left?

_____

Test Prep

8. Which is the greatest capacity?

A. 2,000 mL   **B.** 2 L   **C.** 3 L   **D.** 3,200 mL

9. **Writing in Math** James says that there are 5,000 mL in 50 L. Is he correct? Explain.

_____

_____

PROBLEM-SOLVING STRATEGY   P 12-3
Work Backward

Solve each problem. Write the answer in a complete sentence.

1. This morning 50 mL was poured out of a container of water. Then 1 L of water was added, making the total amount of water 1,500 mL. How much water was in the container before any was poured?

   _____

   _____

2. Marty has $6.25 at the end of the day. Today he bought lunch for $8.50, a bagel for breakfast for $1.25, a newspaper for $2.25, and a necklace for his mother for $37.75. He was paid $12.50 for delivering two boxes of paper to his uncle's office. How much money did Marty have when he started his day?

   _____

   _____

3. Cindy drank 4 c of fruit punch from a pitcher. Jackie drank 2 c and Lauren drank 2 more. There are 2 qt of punch left in the pitcher. How many quarts of punch were there before the girls drank some?

   _____

   _____

4. It took Will 30 min to walk from his house to the grocery store. He was in the store for 45 min, and then walked for 15 min more to his grandmother's house. It was 3 P.M. when he arrived at his grandmother's. What time did Will leave his house?

   _____

   _____

Name_____

Customary Units of Weight

Choose the better estimate for each weight.

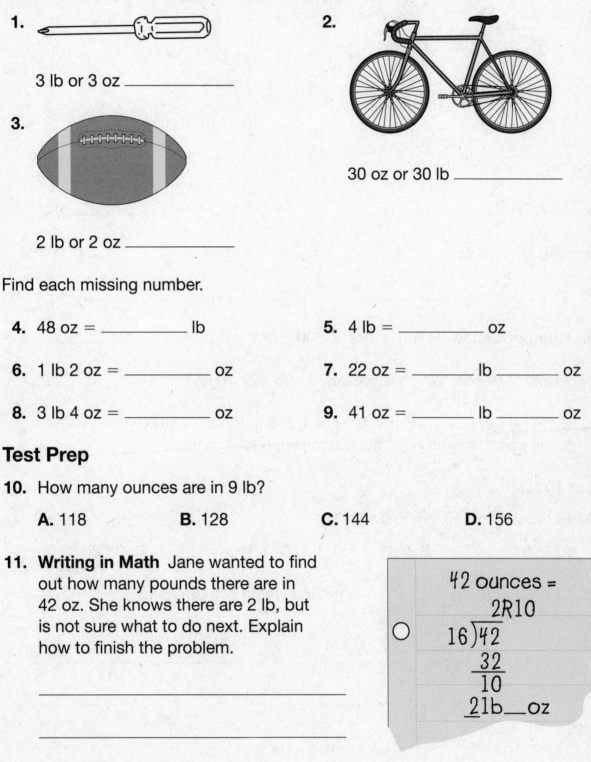

1.

3 lb or 3 oz _____

2.

30 oz or 30 lb _____

3.

2 lb or 2 oz _____

Find each missing number.

4. 48 oz = _____ lb   **5.** 4 lb = _____ oz

6. 1 lb 2 oz = _____ oz   **7.** 22 oz = _____ lb _____ oz

8. 3 lb 4 oz = _____ oz   **9.** 41 oz = _____ lb _____ oz

Test Prep

10. How many ounces are in 9 lb?

     A. 118   **B.** 128   **C.** 144   **D.** 156

11. Writing in Math Jane wanted to find out how many pounds there are in 42 oz. She knows there are 2 lb, but is not sure what to do next. Explain how to finish the problem.

_____

_____

_____

_____

42 ounces =

$$\begin{array}{r} 2\,R10 \\ 16\overline{)42} \\ \underline{32} \\ 10 \end{array}$$

__2 lb___ oz

Grams and Kilograms

Choose the better estimate.

1.

3 g or 3 kg _____

2.

40 kg or 400 g _____

Find each missing number.

3. 40 kg = _____ g

4. 16,000 g = _____ kg

5. 9 kg = _____ g

6. 14 kg = _____ g

7. 4,000 g = _____ kg

8. 7,000 g = _____ kg

9. Number Sense Which is less, 7,500 g or 9 kg? _____

10. Number Sense Which is greater, 8,100 g or 10 kg? _____

11. Eight new crayons weigh a total of 1,200 g. If each crayon is the same weight, how much does each crayon weigh? _____

Test Prep

12. How many grams are in 9 kg 20 g?

A. 110　　　　　**B.** 920　　　　　**C.** 1,100　　　　　**D.** 9,020

13. Writing in Math Explain whether you would use grams or kilograms to weigh a letter.

_____

_____

_____

_____

Temperature

Write each temperature using °F.

1. 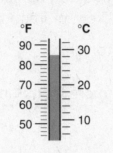 _____

2. _____

Write each temperature using °C.

3. _____

4. _____

Estimate Choose the better outdoor temperature for each activity.

5. jogging

20°C or 40°C

6. sledding

17°F or 40°F

7. gardening

10°C or 25°C

8. If it is 84°F at noon on Monday and 70°F at 11 P.M. on Monday, how much did the temperature drop?

_____

Test Prep

9. Which is the best temperature for snow skiing?

A. 40°C   **B.** 10°C   **C.** 40°F   **D.** 10°F

10. Writing in Math Would you describe the temperature as cold, warm, or hot if it were 35°C? Explain.

_____

_____

_____

Describing Chances

Sarah is an adult with a dog named Fred. Describe each event
as certain, likely, unlikely, or impossible.

1. Fred will sleep tonight. _____

2. Fred will weigh more than Sarah. _____

3. Fred will eat. _____

4. Fred will learn to play the accordion. _____

Describe each spin as certain, impossible,
likely, or unlikely.

5. Spinning a square _____

6. Spinning a triangle _____

7. Spinning an even number _____

8. Spinning an odd number _____

Test Prep

9. Which is the best description of the event that a cat will
   become a doctor?

   A. Likely   **B.** Unlikely   **C.** Certain   **D.** Impossible

10. **Writing in Math** Explain the difference between a likely
    and an unlikely event.

    _____

    _____

    _____

    _____

Fair and Unfair

Use the spinner for 1–4. Give the chance of
each outcome for the spinner.

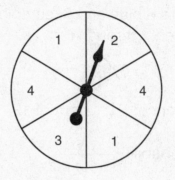

1. Landing on 1: _____ out of _____

2. Landing on 2: _____ out of _____

3. Landing on 3: _____ out of _____

4. Landing on 4: _____ out of _____

5. **Reasoning** In a game with two people, the players take
   turns tossing a six-sided number cube with the numbers 1, 2,
   3, 4, 5, and 6. Player 1 wins if the toss is less than 3. Player 2
   wins if the toss is 3 or more. Is the game fair? Explain.

   _____

   _____

   _____

Test Prep

6. In a spinner with 6 sections, one section is yellow,
   2 sections are blue, and 3 sections are green. Which
   would make the spinner fair?

   A. Change a blue section to yellow   **B.** Change a green section to yellow

   C. Change a blue section to green   **D.** Change the yellow section to green

7. **Writing in Math** Manuel says that a fair game is one in
   which each of the events has the same chance of
   happening. Do you agree? Explain.

   _____

   _____

   _____

Probability

Give the chance and probability of each event.

There are 6 blue and 6 red color cards. Each color has cards
numbered 1 through 6.

1. Drawing a red card

Chance: _____ out of 12

Probability: $\dfrac{=====}{12}$

2. Drawing a card with a 5

Chance: _____ out of _____

Probability: $=====$

_____

A 12-sided number cube has the numbers 1 through 12 on the
sides. Give the probability of tossing

3. an even number. _____

4. a number greater than 9. _____

5. the number 6. _____

6. a 3, 6, 9, or 12. _____

A bag contains 6 marbles: 3 are green, 1 is yellow, and 2 are blue.

7. What is the probability of drawing a green marble? _____

8. What is the probability of drawing an orange marble? _____

Test Prep

9. What is the probability of spinning an even number?

A. 2 out of 4

B. $\frac{1}{4}$

C. $\frac{2}{4}$

D. $\frac{3}{4}$

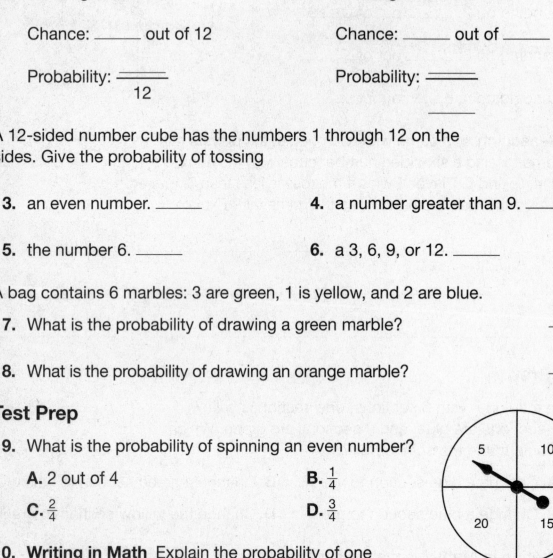

10. Writing in Math Explain the probability of one
event in a fair game with three possible outcomes.

_____

_____

_____

PROBLEM-SOLVING SKILL
Writing to Explain

Write to explain.

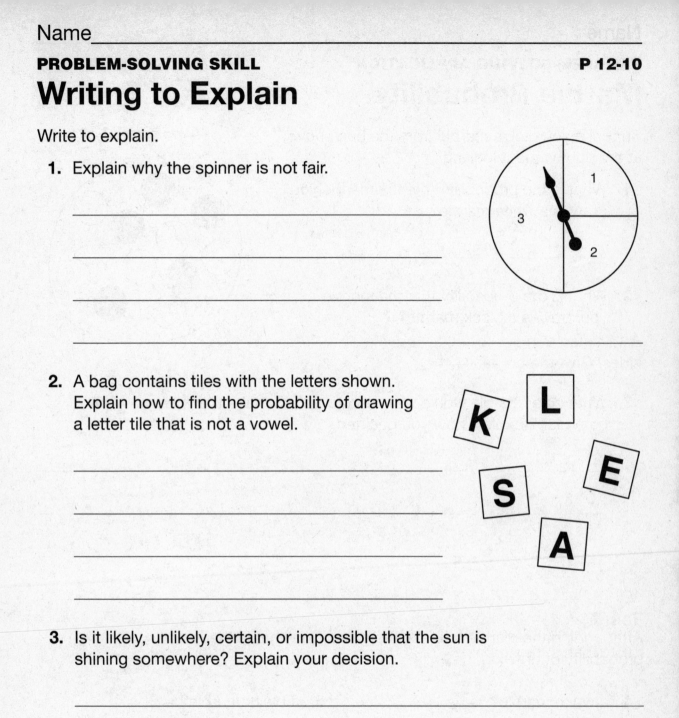

1. Explain why the spinner is not fair.

   _____

   _____

   _____

2. A bag contains tiles with the letters shown. Explain how to find the probability of drawing a letter tile that is not a vowel.

   _____

   _____

   _____

3. Is it likely, unlikely, certain, or impossible that the sun is shining somewhere? Explain your decision.

   _____

   _____

   _____

4. Are you more likely to swim at 30°F or 30°C? Explain how you decided.

   _____

   _____

   _____

PROBLEM-SOLVING APPLICATION
Marble Probability

Suppose you pick a marble from the bag shown
at the right without looking.

1. What is the probability that the marble you
    draw is a white marble?

    _____

2. What is the probability that the marble
    you draw is a black marble?

    _____

3. What color marble would you need to add to make the
    game fair? Explain how you decided.

    _____

    _____

    _____

    _____

After adding the marble to make the game fair, what is the
probability of drawing

4. a white marble? _____   5. a black marble? _____

6. Suppose each marble that is in the bag shown above
    weighs 3 oz. How much will the marbles weigh altogether
    in pounds and ounces? Explain.

    _____

    _____

    _____